continued . . .

"If you think there's nothing new to be said about Buddhism, then take a look at [No Death, No Fear]. Buddhist luminary Thich Nhat Hanh confronts another heady topic ... through parables, stories and his own brand of faith."   —*Body & Soul*

"Zen master Nhat Hanh turns his hard-earned wisdom as a survivor of war, persecution, and exile to the age-old dilemma of what happens when one dies. If the greatest fear is, as he suggests, that one becomes nothing, then how is one to live with this threat of complete annihilation? Using Buddhist parables and anecdotes, Nhat Hanh offers an alternative perspective [that some readers may find] refreshing, especially when it is expressed as calmly and matter-of-factly as Nhat Hanh expresses it."   —*Booklist*

Anger
Chosen as One of the Best Spiritual Books of the Year
by *Spirituality & Health*

"The Buddhist monk addresses the causes of anger and suggests practical tools to embrace and heal it ... Reminding us that small spiritual matters are really large spiritual matters, the author offers wisdom and serenity to comfort readers as they work through anger to a place of 'being peace.' "   —*Library Journal*

"Americans would do well to cool down with the prolific Buddhist monk ... Hanh's suggestions cut refreshingly against the grain. Hanh reminds us that anger begins and ends with ourselves; we may feel that we are mad at our wife and son, but really we are the direct objects of our rage. Hanh doesn't limit his task to discussing anger between families and friends; he also deals with anger between citizens and governments. That expansive vision is not surprising (Hanh, after all, is a Nobel Peace Prize nominee) but it is refreshing, uplifting this book out of the self-absorbed, self-help pile. Like Hanh's other books, this is not weighed down with Buddhist terminology. The appendices ... give it the specifically Buddhist spice that some readers will appreciate. The meat of the book, however, will be accessible to a broad, ecumenical audience."   —*Publishers Weekly*

Going Home:
Jesus and Buddha as Brothers

"Explores the connections between Buddhism and Christianity... a valuable addition to the growing literature on these two religious traditions."
—*Kirkus Reviews*

"[A] beautiful and inspiring gift to all seeking a more meaningful spirituality."
—*Library Journal*

"His book speaks powerfully about the need for tolerance and love in overcoming differences."
—*Publishers Weekly*

Fragrant Palm Leaves:
Journals 1962–1966

"One of the sweetest and most personally revealing of Thich Nhat Hanh's books, it shows the planting of his seeds of remarkable wisdom."
—Jack Kornfield,
author of *A Path with Heart*

"Enlightening... To read his thoughts is to understand the connection between public life and private life, and that such 'interbeing' makes for ecstatic joy."
—Maxine Hong Kingston

"In *Fragrant Palm Leaves*, the venerable poet emerges poignantly disclosing the essence of enlightenment, and also life itself."
—Robert Thurman,
author of *Inner Revolution*

"Informative and inspiring."
—*Publishers Weekly*

OTHER BOOKS BY THICH NHAT HANH

Anger

Being Peace

Be Still and Know

The Blooming of a Lotus

Breathe! You Are Alive

Call Me By My True Names
The Collected Poems of Thich Nhat Hanh

Cultivating the Mind of Love

For a Future to Be Possible

Fragrant Palm Leaves

Going Home

The Heart of the Buddha's Teaching

The Heart of Understanding

Living Buddha, Living Christ

The Long Road Turns to Joy

Love in Action

The Miracle of Mindfulness

Old Path, White Clouds

The Path of Emancipation

Peace Is Every Step

Present Moment, Wonderful Moment

The Sun My Heart

Taming the Tiger Within

Teachings on Love

Touching Peace

Transformation and Healing

NO DEATH, NO FEAR

Comforting Wisdom for Life

THICH NHAT HANH

RIVERHEAD BOOKS

NEW YORK

While the author has made every effort to provide accurate telephone numbers and Internet addresses at the time of publication, neither the publisher nor the author assumes any responsibility for errors, or for changes that occur after publication.

Riverhead Books
Published by The Berkley Publishing Group
A division of Penguin Group (USA) Inc.
375 Hudson Street
New York, New York 10014

First Riverhead hardcover edition: August 2002
First Riverhead trade paperback edition: August 2003
Riverhead trade paperback ISBN: 1-57322-333-6

The Library of Congress has catalogued the Riverhead hardcover edition as follows:

Nhât Hanh, Thích.
No death, no fear: comforting wisdom for life / Thich Nhat Hanh.
p.   cm.
ISBN 1-57322-221-6
1.   Spiritual life—Buddhism.   2.   Buddhism—Doctrines.   I.   Title
BQ4302 .N43   2002   2002021358
294.3'444—dc21

Printed in the United States of America

20 19 18 17 16 15 14

Contents

Foreword

One day, over lunch, my father said to me, "The last time I saw my father, he was in a basket in the living room." We were sitting together at the outdoor dining area of a Mexican restaurant in Key West, Florida. He looked up from his plate of beans and rice, and continued. "My father was a working man. He was a baker; he worked at the co-op in downtown Fitchburg on Leominster Street."

"Tell me about your father's death," I said.

"I don't know anything," he replied.

"What did people say?"

"No one ever said anything. And I never asked." He returned to the silence that I knew all too well.

Sacred Heart Church is two blocks from the house on Sanborn Street in West Fitchburg, Massachusetts, where my father said good-bye to the grandfather I never knew. This was my family's spiritual center when I was growing up. It was a refuge from the daily grind of factory work, arguing spouses, unpaid bills and excess alcohol. This is where I was baptized and where I was sent for my spiritual education.

Every Monday afternoon, after a full day at public school, I reluctantly trudged up Water Street to this building for two hours of catechism.

I still remember the first day, sitting next to my cousin Patty, our fresh new catechism books in hand. As two nuns stood in front of the class, we were told to open our books to page one and to memorize three questions and their three answers. "Who made me?" "God made you." "Why did God make me?" "To love and serve him." "What happens when I die?" "You will live forever with God in Heaven." For the fathers of the church there was no doubt: my soul is eternal and I will live forever.

Reading *The Boston Globe* one Sunday, I was struck by an article about a woman facing the possibility of terminal cancer. The story began, "A Young Life Interrupted . . . Adriana Jenkins doubts God exists. Or fate." "When we die," she says, "we are gone 'ashes to ashes, dust to dust.'" But she imagines death often—the pain, floating upward, looking down on mourners around her hospital bed, a shimmer of light and finally nothing: "off like a light switch." This has become the main alternative for those to whom doubt itself has become a faith; when we die we are gone, we are nothing.

The first funeral I ever attended was in 1968. It was for my mother's father, my grandfather, Sam Rameau. Since then, more than two dozen times, I have stood at the edge of a freshly dug grave, confused, lost and wondering what to think and what to feel about death, asking myself, Are there really only two options to consider, the belief in an eternal soul, or annihilation?

Doubting the belief in an eternal life and dreading the idea of oblivion, I have lived with a dull fear, a kind of cosmic background noise, throughout my life. Which one is true, forever remaining as me or nothingness? Is there an eternal soul and, if there is, will I be in heaven or in hell? Bored forever or in bliss? Alone or with God?

During the Buddha's life, he was questioned many times by scholars and theologians about the opposite philosophies of eternalism and nihilism. When asked if there was an eternal soul, the Buddha replied that there is no permanent self. When asked if we were extinguished into oblivion upon our death, the Buddha said that we are not annihilated. He rejected both of these ideas.

I have a dear friend who is a famous marine biologist. Like many people he believes that when we die we are extinguished forever. He believes this not from a loss of faith or from despair but because of his trust in science. His faith is in the natural world, in the beauty of the unfolding universe around him and in the ability of humans to understand and gain knowledge of that universe.

Thich Nhat Hanh also has an abiding faith in the ability of humans to gain understanding. But his goal is more than the accumulation of scientific knowledge; it is the attainment of liberation and deep personal wisdom based on pure inquiry. Writing in these pages from his own experience, Thich Nhat Hanh proposes a stunning alternative to the opposing philosophies of an eternal soul and nihilism. He tells us: "Since before time you have been free. Birth and death are only doors through which we pass, sacred thresholds on our journey. Birth and death are a game of hide-and-seek. You have never been born and you can never die" and "Our greatest pain is caused by our notions of coming and going." Over and over again, he invites us to practice looking deeply so we can know for ourselves the freedom and joy of the middle way between a permanent self and oblivion. As a poet, he explores the paradoxes of life and gently lifts the veil of illusion, allowing us, maybe for the first time in our lives, to see that our dread of dying is caused by our own misperceptions and misunderstandings.

His insights into life and death are subtle and elegant, and, like all things subtle, best appreciated slowly, in quiet contemplation. Out of the deep wellspring of Thich Nhat Hanh's humanity and compassion comes the balm to heal our hearts.

PRITAM SINGH

One

WHERE DO
WE COME FROM?
WHERE DO
WE GO?

In my hermitage in France there is a bush of japonica, Japanese quince. The bush usually blossoms in the spring, but one winter it had been quite warm and the flower buds had come early. During the night a cold snap arrived and brought with it frost. The next day while doing walking meditation, I noticed that all the buds on the bush had died. I recognized this and thought, *This New Year we will not have enough flowers to decorate the altar of the Buddha.*

A few weeks later the weather became warm again. As I walked in my garden I saw new buds on the japonica manifesting another generation of flowers. I asked the japonica flowers: "Are you the same as the flowers that died in the frost or are you different flowers?" The flowers replied to me: "Thay, we are not the same and we are not different. When conditions are sufficient we manifest and when conditions are not sufficient we go into hiding. It's as simple as that."

This is what the Buddha taught. When conditions are sufficient things manifest. When conditions are no longer sufficient things withdraw. They wait until the moment is right for them to manifest again.

Before giving birth to me, my mother was pregnant with another baby. She had a miscarriage, and that person wasn't born. When I was young I used to ask the question: was that my brother or was that me? Who was trying to manifest at that time? If a baby has been lost it means that conditions were not enough for him to manifest and the child has decided to withdraw in order to wait for better conditions. "I had better withdraw; I'll come back again soon, my dearest." We have to respect his or her will. If you see the world with eyes like this, you will suffer much less. Was it my brother that my mother lost? Or maybe I was about to come out but instead I said, "It isn't time yet," so I withdrew.

Becoming Nothing

Our greatest fear is that when we die we will become nothing. Many of us believe that our entire existence is only a life span beginning the moment we are born or conceived and ending the moment we die. We believe that we are born from nothing and that when we die we become nothing. And so we are filled with fear of annihilation.

The Buddha has a very different understanding of our existence. It is the understanding that birth and death are notions. They are not real. The fact that we think they are true makes a powerful illusion that causes our suffering. The

4

Buddha taught that there is no birth, there is no death; there is no coming, there is no going; there is no same, there is no different; there is no permanent self, there is no annihilation. We only think there is. When we understand that we cannot be destroyed, we are liberated from fear. It is a great relief. We can enjoy life and appreciate it in a new way.

Finding a Lost Loved One

The same thing happens when we lose any of our beloved ones. When conditions are not right to support life, they withdraw. When I lost my mother I suffered a lot. When we are only seven or eight years old it is difficult to think that one day we will lose our mother. Eventually we grow up and we all lose our mothers, but if you know how to practice, when the time comes for the separation you will not suffer too much. You will very quickly realize that your mother is always alive within you.

The day my mother died, I wrote in my journal, "A serious misfortune of my life has arrived." I suffered for more than one year after the passing away of my mother. But one night, in the highlands of Vietnam, I was sleeping in the hut in my hermitage. I dreamed of my mother. I saw myself sitting with her, and we were having a wonderful talk. She looked young and beautiful, her hair flowing down. It was so pleasant to sit there and talk to her as if she had never died. When I woke up it was about two in the morning, and I felt very strongly that I had never lost my mother. The impression that my mother was still with me was very clear. I understood then that the idea of having lost my mother was just an idea. It was obvious in that moment that my mother is always alive in me.

I opened the door and went outside. The entire hillside was bathed in moonlight. It was a hill covered with tea plants, and my hut was set behind the temple halfway up. Walking slowly in the moonlight through the rows of tea plants, I noticed my mother was still with me. She was the moonlight caressing me as she had done so often, very tender, very sweet . . . wonderful! Each time my feet touched the earth I knew my mother was there with me. I knew this body was not mine alone but a living continuation of my mother and my father and my grandparents and great-grandparents. Of all my ancestors. These feet that I saw as "my" feet were actually "our" feet. Together my mother and I were leaving footprints in the damp soil.

From that moment on, the idea that I had lost my mother no longer existed. All I had to do was look at the palm of my hand, feel the breeze on my face or the earth under my feet to remember that my mother is always with me, available at any time.

When you lose a loved one, you suffer. But if you know how to look deeply, you have a chance to realize that his or her nature is truly the nature of no birth, no death. There is manifestation and there is the cessation of manifestation in order to have another manifestation. You have to be very keen and very alert in order to recognize the new manifestations of just one person. But with the practice and with effort you can do it.

So, taking the hand of someone who knows the practice, together do walking meditation. Pay attention to all the leaves, the flowers, the birds and the dewdrops. If you can stop and look deeply, you will be able to recognize your beloved one manifesting again and again in many forms. You will again embrace the joy of life.

Nothing Is Born, Nothing Dies

A French scientist, whose name is Lavoisier, declared, *"Rien ne se crée, rien ne se perd."* "Nothing is born, nothing dies." Although he did not practice as a Buddhist but as a scientist, he found the same truth the Buddha discovered.

Our true nature is the nature of no birth and no death. Only when we touch our true nature can we transcend the fear of non-being, the fear of annihilation.

The Buddha said that when conditions are sufficient something manifests and we say it exists. When one or two conditions fail and the thing does not manifest in the same way, we then say it does not exist. According to the Buddha, to qualify something as existing or not existing is wrong. In reality, there is no such thing as totally existing or totally not existing.

We can see this very easily with television and radio. We may be in a room that has no television or radio. And while we are in that room, we may think that television programs and radio programs do not exist in that room. But all of us know that the space in the room is full of signals. The signals of these programs are filling the air everywhere. We need only one more condition, a radio or a television set, and many forms, colors and sounds will appear. It would have been wrong to say that the signals do not exist because we did not have a radio or television to receive and manifest them. They only seemed not to exist because the causes and conditions were not enough to make the television program manifest. So at that moment, in that room, we say they do not exist. Just because we do not perceive something, it is not correct to say it does not exist. It is only our notion of being and non-being that makes us confused. It is our notion of being and non-being that makes us think something exists or something doesn't exist. Notions of being and non-being cannot be applied to reality.

No Above, No Below

It is like the notion of above and below. To say they exist is also wrong. What is below for us is above for someone else somewhere else. We are sitting here and we say that above is the direction over our head and we think that the opposite direction is below.

People practicing sitting meditation on the other side of the world would not agree that what we call above is above because for them it is below. They are not sitting on their heads. The ideas of above and below always mean to be above something or to be below something, and the ideas of below and above cannot be applied to the reality of the cosmos. These are only concepts to help us relate to our environment. They are concepts that give us a point of reference, but they are not real. Reality is free from all concepts and ideas.

Trapped by a Notion

The Buddha offered an interesting parable concerning ideas and notions. A young tradesman came home and saw that his house had been robbed and burned by bandits. Right outside what was left of the house, there was a small, charred body. He thought the body belonged to his little boy. He did not know that his child was still alive. He did not know that after having burned the house, the bandits had taken the little boy away with them. In his state of confusion, the tradesman believed the body he saw was his son. So he cried, he beat his chest and pulled out his hair in grief. Then he began the cremation ceremony.

This man loved his little boy so much. His son was the raison d'être of his life. He longed for his little boy so much that he could not abandon the little boy's ashes even for one moment. He made a velvet bag and put the ashes inside. He carried the bag with him day and night, and whether he was working or resting, he was never separated from the bag of ashes. One night his son escaped from the robbers. He came to the new house built by his father. He knocked excitedly on the door at two o'clock in the morning. His father called out as he wept, still holding the bag of ashes. "Who is there?"

"It's me, your son!" the boy answered through the door.

"You naughty person, you are not my boy. My child died three months ago. I have his ashes with me right here." The little boy continued to beat on the door and cried and cried. He begged over and over again to come in, but his father continued to refuse him entry. The man held firm to the notion that his little boy was already dead and that this other child was some heartless person who had come to torment him. Finally, the boy left and the father lost his son forever.

The Buddha said that if you get caught in one idea and

consider it to be "the truth," then you miss the chance to know the truth. Even if the truth comes in person and knocks at your door, you will refuse to open your mind. So if you are committed to an idea about truth or to an idea about the conditions necessary for your happiness, be careful. The first Mindfulness Training is about freedom from views:

> *Aware of the suffering created by fanaticism and intolerance,*
> *we are determined not to be idolatrous about or bound to any*
> *doctrine, theory or ideology, even Buddhist ones. Buddhist*
> *teachings are guiding means to help us learn to look deeply and*
> *to develop our understanding and compassion. They are not*
> *doctrines to fight, kill or die for.*

This is a practice to help free us from the tendency to be dogmatic. Our world suffers so much from dogmatic attitudes. The first mindfulness training is important to help us remain free people. Freedom is above all else freedom from our own notions and concepts. If we get caught in our notions and concepts, we can make ourselves suffer and we can also make those we love suffer.

No Coming, No Going

For many of us, our greatest pain is caused by our notions of coming and going. We think that the person we loved came to us from somewhere and has now gone away somewhere. But our true nature is the nature of no coming, no going. We have not come from anywhere, we shall not go anywhere. When conditions are sufficient, we manifest. When conditions are no longer sufficient, we no longer manifest. It does not mean that we do not exist. Like radio waves without a radio, we do not manifest.

Not only do the notions of coming and going not express reality, neither do the notions of being and non-being. We hear these words in the Prajnaparamita Sutra: "Listen Shariputra, all dharmas [phenomena] are marked by emptiness, they are neither produced nor destroyed, neither increasing nor decreasing."

The meaning of emptiness here is very important; it means first of all to be empty of a separate self. Nothing has a separate self, and nothing exists by itself. If we examine things carefully we will see that all phenomena, including ourselves, are composites. We are made up of other parts. We are made of our mother and father, our grandmothers and grandfathers, our body, our feelings, our perceptions, our mental formations, the earth, the sun and innumerable non-self elements.

All these parts depend on causes and conditions. We see that all that has existed, exists or will exist is interconnected and interdependent. All that we see has only manifested because it is a part of something else, of other conditions that make it possible to manifest. All phenomena are neither produced nor destroyed, because they are in a constant process of manifesting.

We may be intelligent enough to understand this, but to understand it intellectually is not enough. To really understand this is to be free from fear. It is to become enlightened. It is to live in inter-being.

We have to practice looking deeply like this to nourish our awakened understanding of no birth and no death in our daily lives. In this way we can realize the wonderful gift of non-fear.

If we just talk about inter-being as a theory, it will not help us. We should ask: "Piece of paper, where do you come from? Who are you? What did you come here to do? Where are you going to go?" We can ask the flame: "Flame, where do you come from and where will you go?" Listen to the reply closely. The flame, the piece of paper, is replying by its presence. We only have to look deeply and we can hear it reply. The flame is saying: "I do not come from anywhere."

That would be the answer of the japonica flowers also. They were not the same and not different. They did not come from anywhere and they did not go anywhere. If there is a baby who is lost, we should not be sad. It is because there were not sufficient causes and conditions for it to arrive at that time. It will come again.

Sadness Lies in Ignorance

The Great Being Avalokiteshvara was a disciple of the Buddha. One day, when he was concentrating in the course of deep understanding, he suddenly saw that everything is without a separate self. Seeing this, he overcame all ignorance, which means he overcame all his suffering.

Looking deeply, we should also see that there is no birth, there is no death; there is no coming, there is no going; there is no being, there is no non-being; there is no same, there is no different.

If we don't learn this practice, it is a terrible waste. We can learn many practices to lessen our sadness and our suffering, but the cream of enlightened wisdom is the insight of no birth, no death. When we have this insight we will have no more fear. We can then enjoy the immense inheritance our ancestors have handed down to us. We should make time to practice these deep and wonderful teachings in our daily lives.

Respecting Our Manifestations

If you look at a friend with the eyes of a meditator, you will see in him or her all generations of their ancestors. You will be very respectful to them and to your own body because you will see their body and your body as the sacred home of all our ancestors.

You will also see that our bodies are the source of all future generations. We will not damage our bodies, because that wouldn't be kind to our descendants. We do not use drugs and we do not eat or drink things that have toxins or that will harm our bodies. This is because our insight of manifestation helps us to live in a healthy way, with clarity and responsibility.

The ideas of inside and outside are also like this. If we say that the Buddha is in us, our parents are in us, our parents are outside of us, or the Buddha is outside of us, these ideas of inside and outside are not applicable. We are caught in ideas, especially ideas of coming and going and being and not being. Only when we rid ourselves of all these ideas can reality appear, the reality of nirvana. When all ideas of is and is not have been extinguished, then reality will manifest itself.

There Is Nothing Like Experience

We can use an example that is easy to understand, of a tangerine or a durian fruit. If there is a person who has never eaten a tangerine or a durian fruit, however many images or metaphors you give him, you cannot describe to him the reality of those fruits. You can only do one thing: give him a direct experience. You cannot say: "Well, the durian is a little bit like the jackfruit or like a papaya." You cannot say anything that will describe the experience of a durian fruit. The durian fruit goes beyond all ideas and notions. The same is true of a tangerine. If you have never eaten a tangerine, however much the other person loves you and wants to help you understand what a tangerine tastes like, they will never succeed by describing it. The reality of the tangerine goes beyond ideas. Nirvana is the same; it is the reality that goes beyond ideas. It is because we have ideas about nirvana that we suffer. Direct experience is the only way.

Two

THE REAL FEAR

We are afraid of death, we are afraid of separation, and we are afraid of nothingness. In the West, people are very afraid of nothingness. When they hear about emptiness, people are also very afraid, but emptiness just means the extinction of ideas. Emptiness is not the opposite of existence. It is not nothingness or annihilation. The idea of existence has to be removed and so does the idea of nonexistence. Emptiness is a tool to help us.

Reality has nothing to do with existence and nonexistence. When Shakespeare says: "To be, or not to be—that is the question," the Buddha answers: "To be or not to be is not the question." To be and not to be are just two ideas opposing each other. But they are not reality, and they do not describe reality.

Not only does awakened insight remove the notion of permanence, but it also removes the notion of impermanence. The notion of emptiness is the same. Emptiness is an instrument, and if you are caught in the notion of emptiness you are lost. The Buddha said in the Ratnakuta Sutra: "If you are caught by the notion of being and non-being, then the notion of emptiness can help you to get free. But if you are caught by the notion of emptiness, there's no hope." The teaching on emptiness is a tool helping you to get the real insight of emptiness, but if you consider the tool as the insight, you just get caught in an idea.

If you have a notion about nirvana, that notion should be removed. Nirvana is empty of all notions, including the notion of nirvana. If you are caught in the notion of nirvana, you have not touched nirvana yet. This deep insight and discovery of the Buddha took him beyond fear, beyond anxiety and suffering and beyond birth and death.

Burning Our Notions

When you have a match, you have the condition to make a fire. If the flame you make with the match lasts long enough, it will also burn up the match. The match gives rise to the fire, but the fire itself burns up the match; the teaching of impermanence is the same. It helps us to have the awakened understanding of impermanence, and the insight of impermanence is what will burn up our idea of impermanence.

We have to go beyond the idea of permanence, but we also have to go beyond the idea of impermanence. Then we can be in touch with nirvana. The same is true of no self. No self is the match; it helps to give rise to the fire of the insight of no self. It is the awakened understanding of no self that will burn up the match of no self.

To practice is not to store up a lot of ideas about no self, impermanence, nirvana or anything else; that is just the work of a cassette recorder. To speak about and distribute ideas is not the study or practice of Buddhism. We can go to a university to study Buddhism, but we will learn only theories and ideas. We want to go beyond ideas to have real insight, which will burn up all our ideas and help us to be free.

Where Is Nirvana?

Look at a quarter. One side of it is called heads, the other side is called tails; they cannot exist without each other. The metal from which they are made contains them both. Without the metal the two sides would not exist. The three elements, heads, tails and metal, inter-are. The metal we could describe as something like nirvana, and the heads and tails as something like the manifestation of impermanence and no self. Through the appearance of either the tails or the heads, you can touch and recognize the presence of the metal. Similarly by looking deeply into the nature of impermanence and no self, you can also touch the nature of nirvana.

The ultimate dimension of nirvana cannot be separated from the historical dimension. When you touch deeply the historical dimension, you also touch the ultimate dimension. The ultimate dimension is always in you. For a practitioner it's very important to touch his or her own nature of impermanence and non-self. If he is successful he will touch the nature of nirvana and attain non-fear. Now he can ride on the waves of birth and death, smiling serenely.

The Historical and Ultimate Dimensions

We look upon reality in our daily lives through the historical dimension, but we can also look upon the same reality in the ultimate dimension. Reality can be manifested in the historical dimension, or it can be manifested in the ultimate dimension. We are similar. We have our daily and historical concerns, but each of us also has our ultimate concerns.

When we look for God or nirvana or the deepest kind of peace, we are concerned about the ultimate. We are not only concerned with the facts of daily life—fame, profit, or our position in society and our projects—but we are also concerned about our true nature. To meditate deeply is to begin to fulfill our ultimate concern.

Waves Are Water

When you look at the surface of the ocean, you can see waves coming up and going down. You can describe these waves in terms of high or low, big or small, more vigorous or less vigorous, more beautiful or less beautiful. You can describe a wave in terms of beginning and end, birth and death. That can be compared to the historical dimension. In the historical dimension, we are concerned with birth and death, more powerful, less powerful, more beautiful, less beautiful, beginning and end and so on.

Looking deeply, we can also see that the waves are at the same time water. A wave may like to seek its own true nature. The wave might suffer from fear, from complexes. A wave may say, "I am not as big as the other waves," "I am oppressed," "I am not as beautiful as the other waves," "I have been born and I have to die." The wave may suffer from these things, these ideas. But if the wave bends down and touches her true nature she will realize that she is water. Then her fear and complexes will disappear.

Water is free from the birth and death of a wave. Water is free from high and low, more beautiful and less beautiful. You can talk in terms of more beautiful or less beautiful, high or low, only in terms of waves. As far as water is concerned, all these concepts are invalid.

Our true nature is the nature of no birth and no death. We do not have to go anywhere in order to touch our true nature. The wave does not have to look for water because she is water. We do not have to look for God, we do not have to look for our ultimate dimension or nirvana, because we are nirvana, we are God.

You are what you are looking for. You are already what you want to become. You can say to the wave, "My dearest wave, you are water. You don't have to go and seek water. Your nature is the nature of nondiscrimination, of no birth, of no death, of no being and of no non-being."

Practice like a wave. Take the time to look deeply into yourself and recognize that your nature is the nature of no-birth and no-death. You can break through to freedom and fearlessness this way. This method of practice will help us to live without fear, and it will help us to die peacefully without regret.

If you carry within yourself deep grief, if you have lost a loved one, if you are inhabited by fear of death, oblivion and annihilation, please take up this teaching and begin to practice it. If you practice well, you will be capable of looking at the cloud, the rose, the pebble or your child with the kind of eyes the Buddha has transmitted to us. You will touch the no-birth, no-death, no-coming, no-going nature of reality. This can liberate you from your fear, from your anxiety and your sorrow. Then you can truly have the kind of peace that will make you strong and stable, smiling as events happen. Living this way will allow you to help many people around you.

Where Were You Before You Were Born?

Sometimes people ask you: "When is your birthday?" But you might ask yourself a more interesting question: "Before that day which is called my birthday, where was I?"

Ask a cloud: "What is your date of birth? Before you were born, where were you?"

If you ask the cloud, "How old are you? Can you give me your date of birth?" you can listen deeply and you may hear a reply. You can imagine the cloud being born. Before being born it was the water on the ocean's surface. Or it was in the river and then it became vapor. It was also the sun because the sun makes the vapor. The wind is there too, helping the water to become a cloud. The cloud does not come from nothing; there has been only a change in form. It is not a birth of something out of nothing.

Sooner or later the cloud will change into rain or snow or ice. If you look deeply into the rain, you can see the cloud. The cloud is not lost; it is transformed into rain, and the rain is transformed into grass and the grass into cows and then to milk and then into the ice cream you eat. Today if you eat an ice cream, give yourself time to look at the ice cream and say:

"Hello, cloud! I recognize you." By doing that, you have insight and understanding into the real nature of the ice cream and the cloud. You can also see the ocean, the river, the heat, the sun, the grass and the cow in the ice cream.

Looking deeply, you do not see a real date of birth and you do not see a real date of death for the cloud. All that happens is that the cloud transforms into rain or snow. There is no real death because there is always a continuation. A cloud continues the ocean, the river and the heat of the sun, and the rain continues the cloud.

Before it was born, the cloud was already there, so today, when you drink a glass of milk or a cup of tea or eat an ice cream, please follow your breathing. Look into the tea or the ice cream and say hello to the cloud.

The Buddha took the time to look deeply and so can we. The Buddha was not a God; he was a human being like us. He suffered, but he practiced, and that is why he overcame his suffering. He had deep understanding, wisdom and compassion. That is why we say he is our teacher and our brother.

If we are afraid of death it is because we have not understood that things do not really die. People say that the Buddha is dead, but it is not true. The Buddha is still alive. If we look around us we can see the Buddha in many forms. The Buddha is in you because you have been able to look deeply and see that things are not really born and that they do not die. We can say that you are a new form of the Buddha, a continuation of the Buddha. Do not underestimate yourself. Look around you a little bit and you will see continuations of the Buddha everywhere.

Am I Yesterday's Me?

I have a photograph of myself when I was a boy of sixteen. Is it a photograph of me? I am not really sure. Who is this boy in the photograph? Is it the same person as me or is it another person? Look deeply before you reply.

There are many people who say that the boy in the photograph and I are the same. If that boy is the same as I am, why does he look so different? Is that boy still alive or has he died? He is not the same as I am and he is also not different. Some people look at that photograph and think the young boy there is no longer around.

A person is made of body, feelings, perceptions, mental formations and consciousness, and all of these have changed in me since that photograph was taken. The body of the boy in the photograph is not the same as my body, now that I am in my seventies. The feelings are different, and the perceptions are very different. It is just as if I am a completely different person from that boy, but if the boy in the photograph did not exist, then I would not exist either.

27

I am a continuation like the rain is the continuation of the cloud. When you look deeply into the photograph, you can see me already as an old man. You do not have to wait fifty-five years. When the lemon tree is in flower, you may not see any fruit, but if you look deeply you can see that the fruit is already there. You just need one more condition to bring forth the lemons: time. Lemons are already there in the lemon tree. Look at the tree and you only see branches, leaves and flowers. But if the lemon tree has time it will express itself in lemons.

Sunflowers in April

If you come to France in April, you will not see any sunflowers. But in July the area around Plum Village has so many sunflowers. Where are the sunflowers in April? If you come to Plum Village in April and look deeply, you will see sunflowers. The farmers have ploughed the land and sown the seed, and the flowers are just waiting for one more condition to show themselves. They are waiting for the warmth of May and June. The sunflowers are there, but they have not fully manifested.

Look deeply at a box of matches. Do you see a flame in it? If you do, you are already enlightened. When we look deeply at a box of matches, we see that the flame is there. It needs only the movement of someone's fingers to manifest. We say: "Dear flame, I know you are there. Now I shall help you express yourself."

The flame has always been in the box of matches and also in the air. If there were no oxygen, the flame could not express itself. If you lit a candle and then covered the flame with something, the flame would go out for lack of oxygen. The survival of the flame depends on oxygen. We cannot say that the flame is inside the box of matches or that the flame is outside the box of matches. The flame is everywhere in space, time and consciousness. The flame is everywhere, waiting to manifest itself, and we are one of the conditions that will help the flame to manifest. However, if we blow on the flame we shall help the flame stop showing itself. Our breath, when we blow on the flame, is a condition that stops the manifestation of the flame in its flame form.

We can light two candles from the match and then blow out the flame on the match. Do you think the flame from the match has died? The flame is not of the nature to be born or to die. The question is, is the flame on the two candles the same flame or two different flames? It is not the same and it is not different. Now another question: is the flame of the match dead? It is both dead and not dead. Its nature is not to die and not to be born. If we leave the candle burning for an hour, will the flame remain the same or become another flame? The wick, the wax and the oxygen are always changing. The part of the wick and the wax that is burning is always transforming. If these things transform, the flame must change too. So the flame is not the same, but it also is not different.

Being Is Not the Opposite of Annihilation

We have an idea of being that it is the opposite of not being. These ideas are no more solid than ideas of right and left. Look at a pen. Can we remove totally its right-hand side? If we use a knife and cut away half of the pen, the part that remains still has a right-hand side. Political parties of the right and the left are immortal—they cannot be removed. As long as there is a right wing, there will be a left wing.

Therefore those on the left of the political spectrum should desire the eternal presence of those on the right. If we remove the right, we have to remove the left at the same time. The Buddha said: "This is because that is. This manifests because that has manifested." This is the Buddha's teaching concerning the creation of the world. It is called the teaching on co-arising. The flame is there because the matches are there. If the matches were not there, the flame would not be there.

The Answer Lies Within

Where does the flame come from? What is its origin? We should look deeply into this question. Do you need to sit in the lotus position to find the answer? I am sure that the answer is already in you. It is just waiting for one more condition to manifest itself. The Buddha said that everyone has Buddha nature in them. Buddha nature is the ability to understand and touch our real nature. The answer is already in you. A teacher cannot give you the answer. A teacher can help you be in touch with the awakened nature, the great understanding and compassion in you. The Buddha invites you to be in touch with the wisdom that is already in you.

Many of us ask: "Where do you go when you die? What happens when you die?" We have friends who have lost someone they love and they ask: "Where is my beloved one now? Where has she gone now?" Philosophers ask: "Where does man come from? Where does the cosmos or the world come from?"

When we look deeply, we see that when all the conditions are sufficient something will manifest. What manifests does not come from anywhere. And when a manifestation ceases, it does not go anywhere.

Creation

"To create" seems to mean that from nothing you suddenly have something. I prefer the use of the expression "manifestation" to the word "creation." Look deeply, and you can understand creation in terms of manifestation. Just as we can understand a cloud as a manifestation of something that has always been there, and rain as the end of the cloud manifestation, we can understand human beings, and even everything around us, as a manifestation that has come from somewhere and will go nowhere. Manifestation is not the opposite of destruction. It simply changes form. Understanding our lives and the cosmos as a manifestation can bring us tremendous peace. If you are grieving over the loss of a loved one, this is an invitation to look deeply and to heal your pain.

There are theologians who have said that God is the ground of being, but what being? It is not the being that is opposed to non-being. If it is the notion of being as opposed to non-being, then that is not God. God transcends all notions, including the notions of creation and destruction. If you look deeply at the notion of creation with the insight of manifestation in mind, you will discover the depth of the teaching on creation. You will discover that nothing is born and nothing dies. There is only manifestation.

Finding Relief

We come to spiritual practice, to a church, a synagogue, a mosque or a meditation center, to find relief from pain and sorrow. But the greatest relief can only be obtained when we are capable of touching the ultimate dimension. In Judaism and in Christianity you may call that dimension God. God is our true nature, the true nature of no birth, no death. That is why if you know how to trust God, to trust your true nature, you will lose your fear and sorrow.

In the beginning you might think of God as a person, but a person is the opposite of a non-person. If you think of God in terms of notions and concepts, you have not yet discovered the reality of God. God transcends all our notions. God is neither a person nor a non-person. A wave in her ignorance is subject to the fear of birth, death, high, low, more or less beautiful, and the jealousy of others. But if a wave is able to touch her true nature, the nature of water, and know that she is water, then all her fear and jealousy will vanish. Water doesn't undergo birth and death, high and low.

Causes

When we look at things like a flower, a table or a house, we think that a house has to be made by someone and a table has to be made by someone in order to be there. Our tendency is to look for a cause that has given birth to the house, a cause that has given birth to the table. We come to the conclusion that the cause of the house must be the house builder: the mason or the carpenter. What is the cause of the table? Who created the table? A carpenter. Who is the creator of the flower? Is it the earth or the farmer or the gardener?

In our minds we think very simply in terms of cause. We think that one cause is enough to bring about what is there. With the practice of looking deeply we find out that one cause can never be enough in order to bring about an effect. The carpenter is not the only cause of the table. If the carpenter does not have things like nails, saw, wood, time and space, food to eat, a father and mother who brought him to life and a multitude of conditions, he would not be able to bring the table into being. The causes are actually infinite.

When we look at the flower we see the same thing. The gardener is only one of the causes. There must be the soil, the sunshine, the cloud, the compost, the seed and many, many other things. If you look deeply, you will see that the whole cosmos has come together in order to help the flower to manifest. If you look deeply into a piece of carrot that you eat at lunch, you will see that the whole cosmos has come together in order to help manifest that piece of carrot.

If we continue to look deeply, we see that a cause is at the same time an effect. The gardener is one of the causes that has helped to manifest the flower, but the gardener is also an effect. The gardener has manifested because of other causes: ancestors, father, mother, teacher, job, society, food, medicine and shelter. Like the carpenter, he is not only a cause, he is also an effect.

Looking deeply, we find that every cause is at the same time an effect. There cannot be something that we can call "pure cause." There are many things we can discover with the practice of looking deeply, and if we are not bound to any dogma or concept we will be free to make our discoveries.

No Pure Cause

When the Buddha was asked, "What is the cause of everything?" he answered with very simple words. He said, "This is, because that is." It means that everything relies on everything else in order to manifest. A flower has to rely on non-flower elements in order to manifest. If you look deeply into the flower, you can recognize non-flower elements. Looking into the flower, you recognize the element sunshine; that is a non-flower element. Without sunshine, a flower cannot manifest. Looking at the flower, you recognize the element cloud; that is a non-flower element. Without clouds, the flower cannot manifest. Other elements are essential, such as minerals, soil, the farmer and so on; a multitude of non-flower elements has come together in order to help the flower manifest.

This is why I prefer the expression "manifestation" to the word "creation." This does not mean that we should not use the word "creation." Of course we can do so, but we should understand that creation does not mean making something out of nothing. Creation is not something that is destroyed and can become nothing. I very much like the term "Wonderful Becoming." It is close to the true meaning of creation.

Three

THE PRACTICE
OF LOOKING
DEEPLY

All authentic practices of the Buddha carry within themselves three essential teachings called the Dharma Seals. These three teachings of the Buddha are impermanence, no self and nirvana. Just as all-important legal documents have the mark or signature of a witness, all genuine practices of the Buddha bear the mark of these three teachings.

If we look into the first Dharma Seal, impermanence, we see that it doesn't just mean that everything changes. By looking into the nature of things, we can see that nothing remains the same for even two consecutive moments. Because nothing remains unchanged from moment to moment, it therefore has no fixed identity or permanent self. So in the teaching of impermanence we always see the lack of an unchanging self. We call this "no self." It is because things are always transforming and have no self that freedom is possible.

The third Dharma Seal is nirvana. This means solidity and freedom, freedom from all ideas and notions. The word "nirvana" literally means "the extinction of all concepts." Looking deeply into impermanence leads to the discovery of

no self. The discovery of no self leads to nirvana. Nirvana is
the Kingdom of God.

Impermanence

The practice and understanding of impermanence is not just
another description of reality. It is a tool that helps us in our
transformation, healing and emancipation.

Impermanence means that everything changes and that
nothing remains the same in any consecutive moments. And
although things change every moment, they still cannot be
accurately described as the same or as different from what
they were a moment ago.

When we bathe in the river today that we bathed in yesterday, is it the same river? Heraclitus said that we couldn't
step into the same river twice. He was right. The water in the
river today is completely different from the water we bathed
in yesterday. Yet it is the same river. When Confucius was
standing on the bank of a river watching it flow by, he said:
"Oh, it flows like that day and night, never ending."

The insight of impermanence helps us to go beyond all
concepts. It helps us to go beyond same and different and
coming and going. It helps us to see that the river is not the
same river but is also not different either. It shows us that the

flame we lit on our bedside candle before we went to bed is not the same flame that is burning the next morning. The flame on the table is not two flames, but it is not one flame either.

Impermanence Makes Everything Possible

We are often sad and suffer a lot when things change, but change and impermanence have a positive side. Thanks to impermanence, everything is possible. Life itself is possible. If a grain of corn is not impermanent, it can never be transformed into a stalk of corn. If the stalk were not impermanent, it could never provide us with the ear of corn we eat. If your daughter is not impermanent, she cannot grow up to become a woman. Then your grandchildren would never manifest. So instead of complaining about impermanence, we should say, "Warm welcome and long live impermanence." We should be happy. When we can see the miracle of impermanence, our sadness and suffering will pass.

Impermanence should also be understood in the light of inter-being. Because all things inter-are, they are constantly influencing one another. It is said that a butterfly's wings flapping on one side of the planet can affect the weather on the other side. Things cannot stay the same because they are influenced by everything else, everything that is not itself.

Practicing Impermanence

All of us can understand impermanence with our intellect, but this is not yet true understanding. Our intellect alone will not lead us to freedom. It will not lead us to enlightenment. When we are solid and we concentrate, we can practice looking deeply. And when we look deeply and see the nature of impermanence, we can then be concentrated on this deep insight. This is how the insight of impermanence becomes part of our being. It becomes our daily experience. We have to maintain the insight of impermanence in order to be able to see and live impermanence all the time. If we can use impermanence as an object of our meditation, we will nourish the understanding of impermanence in such a way that it will live in us every day. With this practice, impermanence becomes a key that opens the door of reality.

We also cannot uncover the insight into impermanence for only a moment and then cover it up and see everything as permanent again. Most of the time we behave with our children as though they will always be at home with us. We never think that in three or four years' time they will leave us to marry and have their own families. Therefore we do not value the moments our children are with us.

I know many parents whose children, when they are eighteen or nineteen years old, leave home and live on their own. The parents lose their children and feel very sorry for themselves. Yet the parents did not value the moments they had with their children. The same is true of husbands and wives. You think that your spouse will be there for the whole of your life, but how can you be so sure? We really have no idea where our partners will be in twenty or thirty years' time or even tomorrow. It is very important to remember every day the practice of impermanence.

Seeing Emotions Through the Eyes of Impermanence

When somebody says something that makes you angry and you wish they would go away, please look deeply with the eyes of impermanence. If he or she were gone, what would you really feel? Would you be happy or would you weep? Practicing this insight can be very helpful. There is a *gatha*, or poem, that we can use to help us:

> *Angry in the ultimate dimension*
> *I close my eyes and look deeply.*
> *Three hundred years from now*
> *Where will you be and where shall I be?*

When we are angry, what do we usually do? We shout, scream, and try to blame someone else for our problems. But looking at anger with the eyes of impermanence, we can stop and breathe. Angry at each other in the ultimate dimension, we close our eyes and look deeply. We try to see three hundred years into the future. What will you be like? What will I be like? Where will you be? Where will I be? We need only to breathe in and out, look at our future and at the other person's future. We do not need to look as far as three hundred years. It could be fifty or sixty years from now when we have both passed away.

Looking at the future, we see that the other person is very precious to us. When we know we can lose them at any moment, we are no longer angry. We want to embrace her or him and say: "How wonderful, you are still alive. I am so happy. How could I be angry with you? Both of us have to die someday, and while we are still alive and together it is foolish to be angry at each other."

The reason we are foolish enough to make ourselves suffer and make the other person suffer is that we forget that we and the other person are impermanent. Someday when we die we will lose all our possessions, our power, our family, everything. Our freedom, peace and joy in the present moment is the most important thing we have. But without an awakened understanding of impermanence, it is not possible to be happy.

Some people do not even want to look at a person when

the person is alive, but when the person dies they write eloquent obituaries and make offerings of flowers. At that point the person has died and cannot really enjoy the fragrance of the flowers anymore. If we really understood and remembered that life was impermanent, we would do everything we could to make the other person happy right here and right now. If we spend twenty-four hours being angry at our beloved, it is because we are ignorant of impermanence.

"Angry in the ultimate dimension/I close my eyes." I close my eyes in order to practice visualization of my beloved one hundred or three hundred years from now. When you visualize yourself and your beloved in three hundred years' time, you just feel so happy that you are alive today and that your dearest is alive today. You open your eyes and all your anger has gone. You open your arms to embrace the other person and you practice: "Breathing in you are alive, breathing out I am so happy." When you close your eyes to visualize yourself and the other person in three hundred years' time, you are practicing the meditation on impermanence. In the ultimate dimension, anger does not exist.

Hatred is also impermanent. Although we may be consumed with hatred at this moment, if we know that hatred is impermanent, we can do something to change it. A practitioner can take resentment and hatred and help it to disappear. Just like with anger, we close our eyes and think, *Where will we be in three hundred years?* With the understanding of hatred in the ultimate dimension, it can evaporate in an instant.

Let Impermanence Nurture Love

Because we are ignorant and forget about impermanence, we don't nurture our love properly. When we first married, our love was great. We thought that if we did not have each other we would not be able to live one more day. Because we did not know how to practice impermanence, after one or two years our love changed to frustration and anger. Now we wonder how we can survive one more day if we have to remain with the person we once loved so much. We decide there is no alternative: we want a divorce. If we live with the understanding of impermanence, we will cultivate and nurture our love. Only then will it last. You have to nourish and look after your love for it to grow.

No Self

Impermanence is looking at reality from the point of view of time. No self is looking at reality from the point of view of space. They are two sides of reality. No self is a manifestation of impermanence, and impermanence is a manifestation of no self. If things are impermanent, they are without a separate self. If things are without a separate self, they are impermanent. Impermanence means being transformed at every moment. This is reality. And since there is nothing unchanging, how can there be a permanent self, a separate self? When we say "self," we mean something that is always itself, unchanging day after day. But nothing is like that. Our body is impermanent, our emotions are impermanent and our perceptions are impermanent. Our anger, our sadness, our love, our hatred and our consciousness are also impermanent.

So what permanent thing is there that we can call a self? The piece of paper on which these words are written does not have a separate self. It can only be present when the clouds, the forest, the sun, the earth, the people who make the paper, and the machines are present. If those things are not present, the paper cannot be present. And if we burn the paper, where is the self of paper?

Nothing can exist by itself alone. It has to depend on every other thing. That is called inter-being. To be means to inter-be. The paper inter-is with the sunshine and with the forest. The flower cannot exist by itself alone; it has to inter-be with soil, rain, weeds and insects. There is no being; there is only inter-being.

Looking deeply into a flower, we see that the flower is

made of non-flower elements. We can describe the flower as being full of everything. There is nothing that is not present in the flower. We see sunshine, we see the rain, we see clouds, we see the earth, and we also see time and space in the flower. A flower, like everything else, is made entirely of non-flower elements. The whole cosmos has come together in order to help the flower manifest herself. The flower is full of everything except one thing: a separate self, a separate identity.

The flower cannot be by herself alone. The flower has to inter-be with the sunshine, the cloud and everything in the cosmos. If we understand being in terms of inter-being, then we are much closer to the truth. Inter-being is not being and it is not non-being. Inter-being means being empty of a separate identity, empty of a separate self.

No self also means emptiness, a technical term in Buddhism that means the absence of a separate self. We are of the nature of no self, but that does not mean that we are not here. It does not mean that nothing exists. A glass can be empty or full of tea, but in order to be either empty or full, the glass has to be there. So emptiness does not mean non-being, and it does not mean being either. It transcends all concepts. If you touch deeply the nature of impermanence, no self and inter-being, you touch the ultimate dimension, the nature of nirvana.

Who Are We?

We think of our body as our self or belonging to our self. We think of our body as me or mine. But if you look deeply, you see that your body is also the body of your ancestors, of your parents, of your children and of their children. So it is not a "me," it is not a "mine." Your body is full of everything else—limitless non-body elements—except one thing: a separate existence.

Impermanence has to be seen in the light of emptiness, of inter-being and of non-self. These things are not negative. Emptiness is wonderful. Nagarjuna, the famous Buddhist teacher of the second century, said, "Thanks to emptiness, everything is possible."

You can see non-self in impermanence, and impermanence in non-self. You can say that impermanence is non-self seen from the angle of time, and non-self is impermanence seen from the angle of space. They are the same thing. That is why impermanence and non-self inter-are. If you do not see impermanence in non-self, that is not non-self. If you do not see non-self in impermanence, that's not really impermanence. But that is not all. You have to see nirvana in impermanence and you have to see nirvana in non-self. If I draw a line, on one side there will be impermanence and non-self, on the other side there will be nirvana. That line may be helpful, although it could also be misleading. Nirvana means going beyond all concepts, even the concepts of no self and impermanence. If we have nirvana in no self and in impermanence it means that we are not caught in no self and impermanence as ideas.

Clones: No Permanent Self

If you take three cells from my body to make clones and make three children from these cells, all of them will have the genetic inheritance of my blood family and myself.

But we all have one more inheritance. The body we inherit from our family is nature. We also have an inheritance from our environment. That is nurture. So imagine that we put these three clones into three different environments. If one of the children is put into an environment of drugs and gambling, he will probably become a person who enjoys drugs and gambling. He will not be a Buddhist monk like I am now. If you put another cloned child into an environment of business and send him to a business school, he will probably become a businessman. This would occur even though the clones will all have the same genetic inheritance as I do. But I have been penetrated by the Buddha dharma. The teachings of the Buddha and the practice will not be watered by business school. The seeds of selling, buying and business will be watered. That clone may become a business-man. Although the eyes, nose and ears will look just like me, this clone will be nothing like me.

Let us say that we allow the third clone to become a monk. We put him in the Deer Park Monastery to be brought up by monks and nuns. Every day he hears the sutras and does walking meditation. That child will be more like the monk I am today.

Nurture is extremely important. If you make three clones or three thousand clones, the particular manifestation of the clone depends on the conditions that nurture that clone; the thinking, the love, the hate, the studying and the work that surround him or her. Imagine if there are people who are afraid to let me go and they say: "Please give us a cell for us to clone." If I were to agree, I would also have to say: "Well, please let that clone be in a monastery like the Deer Park Monastery in California, or Maple Forest Monastery in Vermont; otherwise, he will suffer."

Nirvana

Impermanence and no self are not rules to follow given to us by the Buddha. They are keys to open the door of reality. The idea of permanence is wrong, so the teaching on imper-manence helps us correct our view of permanence. If we get caught in the idea of impermanence, we have not realized nirvana. The idea of self is wrong, so we use the idea of non-self to cure it. If we are caught in the idea of non-self, then that is not good for us either. Impermanence and no self are keys to the practice. They are not absolute truths. We do not die for them or kill for them.

In Buddhism there are no ideas or prejudices that we kill for. We do not kill people simply because they do not accept our religion. The teachings of the Buddha are skillful means; they are not absolute truth. So we have to say that impermanence and no self are skillful means to help us come toward the truth; they are not absolute truth. The Buddha said: "My teachings are a finger pointing to the moon. Do not get caught in thinking that the finger is the moon. It is because of the finger that you can see the moon."

No self and impermanence are means to understand the truth; they are not the truth itself. They are instruments; they are not the ultimate truth. Impermanence is not a doctrine that you should feel you have to die for. You would never put someone in prison because they contradict you. You are not using one concept against another concept. These means are to lead us to the ultimate truth. Buddhism is a skillful path to help us; it is not a path of fanatics. Buddhists can never go to war, shedding blood and killing thousands of people on behalf of religion.

Because impermanence contains within herself the nature

of nirvana, you are safe from being caught in an idea. When you study and practice this teaching, you free yourself from notions and concepts, including the concept of permanence and impermanence. This way, we arrive at freedom from suffering and fear. This is nirvana, the kingdom of God.

Extinction of Concept

We are scared because of our notions of birth and death, increasing and decreasing, being and non-being. Nirvana means extinction of all notions and ideas. If we can become free from these notions, we can touch the peace of our true nature.

There are eight basic concepts that serve to fuel our fear. They are the notions of birth and death, coming and going, the same and different, being and non-being. These notions keep us from being happy. The teaching given to counteract these notions is called "the eight no's," which are no birth, no death, no coming, no going, not the same, not different, no being, no non-being.

Ending Notions of Happiness

Each of us has a notion of how we can be happy. It would be very helpful if we took the time to reconsider our notions of happiness. We could make a list of what we think we need to be happy: "I can only be happy if . . ." Write down the things you want and the things you do not want. Where did these ideas come from? Are they reality? Or are they only your notions? If you are committed to a particular notion of happiness, you do not have much chance to be happy.

Happiness arrives from many directions. If you have a notion that it comes only from one direction, you will miss all of these other opportunities because you want happiness to come only from the direction you want. You say, "I would rather die than marry anyone but her. I would rather die than lose my job, my reputation. I cannot be happy if I don't get that degree or that promotion or that house." You have put many conditions on your happiness. And then, even if you do have all your conditions met, you still won't be happy. You will just keep creating new conditions for your happiness. You will still want the higher degree, the better job and the more beautiful house.

A government can also believe that they know the only way to make a nation prosper and be happy. That government and nation may commit itself to that ideology for one hundred years or more. During that time its citizens can suffer so much. Anyone who disagrees or dares to speak against the government's ideas will be locked up. They might even be considered insane. You can transform your nation into a prison because you are committed to an ideology.

Please remember that your notions of happiness may be very dangerous. The Buddha said happiness can only be possible in the here and now. So go back and examine deeply your notions and ideas of happiness. You may recognize that the conditions of happiness that are already there in your life are enough. Then happiness can be instantly yours.

Four

TRANSFORMING GRIEF AND FEAR

THE CLOUD

As a free person I can always come and go,
Not caught in ideas of is and is not.
Not caught in ideas of being and non-being
Let your steps be leisurely.
Waxing or waning the moon is always the moon
The wind is still flying. Can you feel it my dear?
Bringing the rain from afar to nourish the nearby cloud
Drops of sunshine fall from on high to earth below
And the lap of earth touches the clear vault of the sky.

—THICH NHAT HANH

On a beautiful sunny day, you look up into the sky and see a nice, puffy cloud floating through. You admire its shape, the way the light falls upon its many folds and the shadow it casts on the green field. You fall in love with this cloud. You want it to stay with you and keep you happy. But then the shape and color change. More clouds join with it, the sky becomes dark, and it begins to rain. The cloud is no longer apparent to you. It has become rain. You begin to cry for the return of your beloved cloud.

You would not cry if you knew that by looking deeply into the rain you would still see the cloud.

In Buddhism there is the teaching of signlessness (*animitta*). "Sign" means the outer form or appearance of things. The practice of signlessness is the practice of not being fooled by the outer form or the appearance of things. When we understand *animitta*, we understand that appearance is not all of reality.

When a cloud transforms itself into rain you can look deeply into the rain and see that the cloud is still there, laughing and smiling at you. This makes you happy, and you are able to stop crying because you are no longer attached to the appearance of the cloud. If you are struck down by your grief and you continue to cry for a long time, it is because you have been left behind, caught in the form or sign of the cloud. You are caught in an appearance from the past and you are not able to see the new form. You have not been able to follow the cloud as it transforms into rain or snow.

If you have lost someone and if you have cried so very much, please accept the invitation of the Buddha. Look deeply and recognize that the nature of your beloved is the nature of no birth, no death, no coming, no going. This is the teaching of the Buddha concerning our true nature.

Transformation

Let us look into the birth of a cloud. You can visualize the heat, you can see the vapor, you can see the formation of the cloud in the sky. You know where the cloud has come from. We can understand the conditions that have helped the cloud to manifest in the sky. Our observation and our practice of looking deeply can help. Science can also tell us about the formation of a cloud, the journey of a cloud and the adventure of a cloud.

If you were to love a cloud, with this insight you would know that the cloud is impermanent. If you love a human being you can also know that he or she is impermanent. If you were to become attached to a cloud you would have to be very careful. You know that, according to the law of impermanence, very soon the cloud will become something else. It might become rain.

You might say to the cloud, "Darling cloud, I know you are there and I also know that one day you will die. I also must die. You will become something else, someone else. I know you will continue your journey, but I shall have to look deeply in order to recognize your continuation so that I will not suffer so much."

If you forget about impermanence and are attached to the cloud, when the time comes for the cloud to be transformed into rain, you will cry, "Oh dear, my cloud is no longer there. How can I survive without her?"

But if you practice looking deeply, you can see the cloud in new forms like the mist or the rain. The rain is smiling, singing, falling down, full of life, full of beauty. Yet because of your forgetfulness you are not capable of recognizing the presence of the cloud in this new manifestation. You are caught in grief. You keep crying and crying and meanwhile the rain is calling you, "Darling, darling, I am here, recognize me!" But you ignore the rain while all the time the rain is the continuation of the cloud. In fact the rain is the cloud herself.

When you look at the cloud, you might like to be like a cloud floating freely in the sky. How wonderful it would be to be a cloud floating in the sky! You would have such a feeling of freedom. When you look at the rain falling, singing and making music, you might also long to be the rain. The rain is nourishing all the vegetation and the lives of innumerable beings. How wonderful it is to be the rain.

Do you think the rain and the cloud are the same or different? The snow on the top of a mountain is so white, so immaculate, so beautiful. It is so enchanting that you might like to see yourself as being like the snow. Sometimes when you look at the water flowing in the creek, you see the stream so crystal pure and beautiful that you may like to be like the water, always flowing. Cloud, rain, snow and water. Are they four different things? Or are they really the same reality, sharing the same ground of being?

No Fear

In chemistry we would call the ground of being of water H_2O: two hydrogen atoms and an oxygen atom. From this ground of being, a molecule, many things can manifest: clouds, rain, snow, water. It is wonderful to be a cloud, but it is also wonderful to be the rain. It is also wonderful to be the snow or water. If the cloud remembers this, then when the cloud is about to transform and continue in the form of rain, it will not be so frightened. It will remember that to be a cloud is wonderful, but to be the rain falling down is also wonderful.

When the cloud is not caught in the idea of birth and death, or being and non-being, there is no fear. By learning from the cloud, we can nurture our non-fear. Non-fear is the ground of true well-being. As long as fear is in us, happiness cannot be perfect.

When you practice looking deeply, you see your true nature of no birth, no death; no being, no non-being; no coming, no going; no same, no different. When you see this, you are free from fear. You are free from craving and free from jealousy. No fear is the ultimate joy. When you have the insight of no fear, you are free. And like the great beings, you ride serenely on the waves of birth and death.

Manifesting and Hiding

The true nature of all things is not to be born, not to die, not to arrive and not to depart. My true nature is the nature of no coming and no going. When there are sufficient conditions, I manifest, and when the conditions are no longer sufficient, I hide. I do not go anywhere. Where would I go? I simply hide.

If your dear one has just died, you may have a difficult time overcoming your loss. You may be crying all the time. But look deeply. There is a divine medicine to help you overcome your pain, to see that your dear one is not born and does not die, does not come and does not go.

It is only because of our misunderstanding that we think the person we love no longer exists after they "pass away." This is because we are attached to one of the forms, one of the many manifestations of that person. When that form is gone, we suffer and feel sad.

The person we love is still there. He is around us, within us and smiling at us. In our delusion we cannot recognize him, and we say: "He no longer is." We ask over and over, "Where are you? Why did you leave me all alone?" Our pain is great because of our misunderstanding. But the cloud is not lost.

Our beloved is not lost. The cloud is manifesting in a different form. Our beloved is manifesting in a different form. If we can understand this, then we will suffer much less.

Taking New Forms

When we lose someone we love, we should remember that the person has not become nothing. "Something" cannot become "nothing," and "nothing" cannot become "something." Science can help us understand this, because matter cannot be destroyed—it can become energy. And energy can become matter, but it cannot be destroyed. In the same way, our beloved was not destroyed; she has just taken on another form. That form may be a cloud, a child or the breeze. We can see our loved one in everything. And smiling, we can say, "Dear one, I know you are there very close to me. I know that your nature is the nature of no birth and no death. I know that I have not lost you; you are always with me."

If you look deeply at every moment of your daily life, you will see that person. Practicing like this, you will be able to overcome your grief. The same is true with your mother or your father. Their true nature is the nature of not born, not dying, not arriving and not departing. In reality, you have not lost anyone who has died.

The Story of the River and the Clouds

There is a story I like to tell about a river that followed the clouds. There is a little stream that comes from a mountain spring. It is very small and young and wants to reach the sea as quickly as possible. It does not know how to dwell peacefully in the present moment. It is in a hurry because it is so young. It has not realized the practice of "I am home, I have arrived," so it flows down the mountain, reaches the plains and becomes a river.

As a river it has to go more slowly. This is irritating because it is afraid that it will never get to the sea. But since it is forced to go more slowly, its waters become more still. Its surface begins to reflect the clouds in the sky—pink clouds, silver clouds, white clouds. There are so many wonderful shapes. All day it follows the clouds. It becomes attached to the beautiful clouds. So the river suffers because the clouds are impermanent. They are always moving with the wind, leaving the river to go off somewhere else. How the river suffers! The river tries over and over to hold on to the clouds. It is sad that the clouds will not stay with it and stand still.

One day a stormy wind blew all the clouds away. The vault of the sky was very clear blue and empty. How the river despaired. It no longer had a cloud to follow. There was not a cloud in the sky. The vast expanse of blue brought despair into the river's heart. "What is there to live for without the clouds? What is there to live for without my beloved one?" The river wanted to die, but how could a river kill itself? All night long it wept.

That night the river had a chance to listen to itself crying. The sound of its weeping was the sound of its own waves lapping on the shore. When it was able to come back to itself and hear its own crying, it had a very wonderful insight. It realized that its own nature was also the nature of the cloud. It was the cloud. The cloud lay in the depths of its own being. Just like the river, the cloud was grounded in water. The cloud was made of water. *So why*, the river thought, *do I need to run after the cloud? I only need to run after the cloud if I am not the cloud.*

That night of utter loneliness and depression helped the river to wake up and see that it was also the cloud. That morning the blue emptiness of the sky, which had made the river feel so lonely, was now something new and very wonderful, clear and bright. The blueness of the sky was reflecting the newfound freedom and innocence of the river. It knew that the vault of the sky was the home of all the clouds and no cloud could exist outside the vault of the sky. The river understood that the nature of the cloud was not to arrive and not to depart, so why should the river cry? Why should it weep as if it had been torn from the cloud?

The river had another insight that morning. It saw the no-birth, no-death nature of the sky. This made the river very peaceful and quiet. It began to welcome and reflect the sky. Before that, it had not reflected the sky, it had only reflected the clouds. Now the sky was always there for the river, day and night. Before, the river had not wanted to be in touch with the true nature of things. It had only wanted to be in touch with change, with birth and death. Now that it had been in touch with the vault of the sky, it became very peaceful and quiet. It had never felt so much peace.

That afternoon when the clouds came back, the river was no longer attached to any particular one of them. There was no cloud it felt to be its own special cloud. It smiled at every cloud as it passed. It welcomed and loved every cloud.

Now the river felt the special joy of equanimity. It was not partial to any particular cloud or in the grip of any particular cloud. It loved them all. It could enjoy being with and reflecting every cloud that came through the sky. When a cloud left it, the river said, "Good-bye. See you again soon," and it felt very light at heart. It knew that the cloud would return to it after it became rain or snow.

The river was free. It did not feel it even needed to run to the sea anymore. That night a full moon rose and shone into the depths of the river. The moon, the river and the water practiced meditation together. The river enjoyed the present moment in freedom. It was liberated from all sorrow.

When we chase an object, trying to grab it, we suffer. And when there is no object to run after, we also suffer. If

you have been a river, if you have run after the clouds, suffered, cried and been lonely, please hold the hand of a friend.
Looking deeply together, you can see that what you were
looking for has always been there. In fact it is you, yourself.

You are what you want to become. Why search anymore? You are a wonderful manifestation. The whole universe has come together to make your existence possible.
There is nothing that is not you. The kingdom of God, the
Pure Land, nirvana, happiness and liberation are all you.

The Same Body?

Suppose we practice cloning, and every cell in our body is
made into a new body. Does that mean that one soul can become many souls? One person can become many people? Are
all those new people the same or different?

Science has already advanced to the point where it can
perform cloning of animals. It is possible that this can be
done with human beings also. If, for example, we take three
cells from my body and we make three clones, will those
three clones plus myself make four people or one person?
When the clones are made, I might already be quite old and
the three clones would be very young. So am I and those
three people the same or different?

If we practice meditation, we can look deeply with the

power of mindfulness, the energy of concentration and the energy of insight. Then we are able to see things much more deeply and clearly. The Buddha is someone who practiced like that, and he shared the insight he had with us. We also practice like the Buddha, and with a little effort we will have insight like the Buddha had.

First we should look deeply into the idea of the same and different. When we ask the Buddha: "Are this body and the other three clones the same or different?" the Buddha will say, "They are not the same and they are not different."

Impermanence means something is always changing. We think that our body is permanent. In fact, birth and death are taking place in our body all the time. At every moment many cells are dying and many cells are being born.

We have the illusion that our bodies are always our bodies. You were born a baby. Your mother took a picture of you when you were small, and now you have grown into a man or woman. Do you think you are the same person as that tiny baby, or are you different?

We think that at five years old it is our bodies and at fifty years old it is our bodies. But it is wrong to think that it is the same body. If you have a family photo album, please look at it and you will see what you looked like when you were six years old and what you look like now at sixty. You will see that those two people look very different. They are different. But in another sense they are not different. If there were not the six-year-old, there would not be the sixty-year-old. They are not the same and they are not different. Impermanence is the explanation for this puzzle.

After one in- and out-breath we have already become a different person. From the moment we began reading this book until this moment, there have been many changes within our bodies and within our consciousnesses. Many cells have died; many new cells have been born. The same is true of our consciousness. Thoughts come and go, feelings are born and die. Manifestation and the cessation of manifestation are constantly taking place. We do not remain the same in two consecutive moments. The same is true of the river, the flame, the cloud or the sunflower.

Conditions

Looking deeply into a box of matches, you can see the flame. The flame has not manifested, but as a meditator you can see the flame. All the conditions are sufficient for the flame to manifest. There is wood, sulfur, a rough surface and my hands. So when I strike the match and the flame appears I would not call that the birth of a flame. I would call it a manifestation of a flame.

The Buddha said that when conditions are sufficient you manifest yourself. When conditions are no longer sufficient, you stop the manifestation in order to manifest in other forms, with other conditions.

Manifesting from Something

What do you think birth is? Most of us think birth means that something begins to exist where something didn't exist before. In our mind we have the concept that birth means that from nothing you suddenly become something; from no one you suddenly become someone. Most of us would define birth like that. Looking deeply, we see that this definition is not sound. From nothing, you cannot become something. From no one, you can never become someone.

Before your so-called birthday, you were already there, in your mother. So that moment of childbirth is only a moment of continuation. Look and see if you can find the moment that you became something from nothing. Was it at the moment of conception in the womb of your mother? That is not correct either, because before that there had been something else, maybe half in your father, half in your mother; maybe one third in your father, one third in your mother, one third in the cosmos. There were many "somethings" that were already there. If something existed already, it does not need to be born. The time when a mother is in labor and then gives birth is not really the moment of birth; it is just a moment of the coming into the world from the womb.

In Zen we like to ask the question, "What did your face look like before your grandmother was born?" Ask yourself this question and you will begin to see your own continuation. You will see that you have always been there. The moment of your conception is a moment of continuation, of manifesting in another form. If you keep looking you will see that instead of birth and death, there is only continuing transformation.

Where Does the Flame Come From?

I can say to the flame, "Dear flame, please manifest yourself." As I strike the match, the flame complies. But I would also like to ask her, "Where have you come from?"

The flame would say this: "Dear Thay, I come from nowhere and I go nowhere. When conditions are sufficient, I manifest." That is the truth of the nature of no coming, no going.

Let us practice looking deeply into the nature of the flame of a candle. Is it the same flame as the flame of the match that lit it? Or is it a different flame? If we maintain this flame for one hour, the flame will burn lower on the candle. It may appear to be the same flame, but that is only our perception. In fact there are multitudes of flames succeeding one another in every instant. They give the impression that it is always the same flame, but it is not. The fuel is different, the oxygen is different. The room has changed, and so the conditions are different. Therefore the flame is not exactly the same.

It does not take much time for the flame to change because in one second the flame is nourished by the wax and oxygen in the first part of the candle. The next moment, the oxygen and the wax are being burned away and new fuel, new wax and oxygen, are now burning. It is not the same fuel, so it is not the same flame. When the candle becomes shorter, you see that it has consumed this much wax and that much oxygen, so you know that the flame is changing all the time. Just like us, the flame does not remain the same in two consecutive moments.

Looking at just one flame you see already the nature of being neither the same nor different. Underneath our impression of being the same, there is the nature of impermanence. Nothing can remain the same in two consecutive moments. This applies to a human being, a cloud, to everything. If you say that the flame burning on the candle ten minutes ago is the same as the flame you see now, this is not correct. If you say there are one thousand different flames succeeding each other, this is not correct either. The true nature of the flame is the nature of neither the same nor different. If we can move through the illusion of same and different, we can change a lot of suffering into joy.

Impressions

In the sutras there is an excellent example. In the darkness one person holds a torch and draws a circle of fire. Another person, standing a little bit away, has the impression that there is a fire circle. But there is no circle, there are only dots of fire that succeed each other and give the impression of a fire circle. This is like the illusion of fixed identity and the illusion of permanence. The fire circle is an idea. It cannot be applied to reality, and it cannot describe the true reality. If you analyze the fire circle you will see that there are millions of instances moving in quick succession that give the impression that there is a fire circle.

When we film someone dancing, we are taking many pictures of that person dancing. We take so many pictures and then when we project these frames one after another, we have the impression that there is fluid movement. But in fact these are only innumerable still pictures, one succeeding another.

When we look at someone, we have the impression that there is a permanent self or entity. We think that this morning I recognized this identity and this evening, when I look, I will recognize that same entity. If I travel somewhere else and come back ten years later I will also recognize the same entity. That is an illusion.

There's a very funny story in the sutras. A woman left a saucepan of milk with her neighbor, saying: "Please keep it for me; I shall come back in two or three days." There was no refrigeration, so the milk curdled and became a kind of cheese. When the woman came back she said: "Where's my milk? I left milk behind, not cheese, so this is not my milk here." The Buddha said that this person had not understood impermanence. Milk will become yogurt or cheese if you leave it for a few days. The person wanted only the milk of five days ago and refused to take the cheese. Do you think that milk and cheese are the same or different? They are neither the same nor different, but it takes several days for the milk to become cheese. With the insight of impermanence we can see the truth about the universe and all phenomena, the true nature of being neither the same nor different.

We presume that things remain the same forever, but in reality nothing remains the same in two consecutive moments. That is why the notion of a fixed identity is also an illusion, an idea that cannot be applied to reality. There is a stream of manifestation, yes, and you can assign to it a name, like the Mississippi River. Although the name does not change, the reality does. You have the impression that the river is always there for you, but the water in it is not the same even after just one moment. Philosophers have said that you can never bathe twice in the same river. This is the nature of impermanence confirmed, not only by the Buddha, but by Confucius and Heraclitus and many other wise people who knew how to look deeply into the nature of reality.

St. Francis and the Almond Tree

One day, while doing walking meditation during winter in his garden, St. Francis of Assisi saw a bare almond tree. He approached the almond tree and, as he practiced breathing in and out, asked the almond tree to tell him about God. Suddenly the almond tree was covered with blossoms. I believe the story to be true because such a contemplative could see into the depth of reality. He did not need to have the warmth of spring in order to realize that the almond blossoms were already there.

I invite you to look at a box of matches with the eyes of St. Francis, the eyes of the Buddha. You do have those eyes. Can you see the flame already in the box of matches? It has not manifested but it is there somewhere. Looking deeply, you can already see the flame. All conditions are there for the flame to manifest, except one—a movement of your fingers. You can furnish that last condition and see the flame manifesting.

When you strike a match, please do it very mindfully. Observe all the conditions. Ask the flame, "Dear little flame, where have you come from?" When you extinguish it, ask, "Where have you gone to?" We think the flame, which was born a moment ago, is now going to die. Is there any place separate from us in space that the flame has gone to? I don't think so.

The Buddha said that there is no coming; there is no going. These are questions philosophers have asked many times and have used so much paper, ink and saliva to try to answer. Looking deeply with your Buddha eyes, you can find the answer.

Suchness

Reality, as it is, is called suchness. Suchness means, "it is like that." You cannot describe it in terms of notions, especially notions of birth and death, being and non-being, coming and going. No word, no idea, no notion can describe reality: the reality of a table, the reality of a flower, the reality of a house, the reality of a living being.

Sometimes you are angry with your father and you say, "I don't want anything to do with him!" What a declaration! You don't know that you and your father belong to the same reality; you are his continuation, you are he. Look into whether you are the same as your father or different from him. Our true nature is the nature of not the same, not different. You and your father are not the same; and you are not different.

When you help the flame to manifest by striking the match, look deeply and you can see that it comes from nowhere, and it goes nowhere. Use the flame on the match to light a candle. Is the flame of the candle the same as the flame of the match or different? If you have a second candle and light it too, you can ask if the three flames are the same or different.

Looking into a flame of one candle, we can see in this very flame that the idea of "neither the same nor different" applies not only to the flames of the two different candles but also to the one flame that lit them both. This flame is not the same and is not different because each moment of that flame is unique. The moment that comes next is a moment when the flame manifests itself in a different way.

The manifestation of something or someone does not rely on one condition alone; it relies on many conditions. So, the idea that one cause can bring about the effect is not correct. One cause is never enough to help something manifest.

While we were contemplating the flame we did not look deeply enough to see all the conditions. We know that the flame is nourished by the matchstick, by the wood and by fuel. It is true that nothing can survive without fuel, but the fuel is only one element, one condition. The flame can manifest itself only when all the elements are there. If there is no oxygen in the air, the flame cannot appear for very long. The flame relies on the wood, on the wick, on oxygen. The flame is already there in the matchbox. It does not need to be born, it only needs to manifest when the conditions are right.

We may only be a boy or a girl of twelve years old and do not now have children of our own. But in our person, all the causes and conditions for the manifestation of children and grandchildren are there. It's just a matter of time and conditions.

A SHEET OF PAPER

No coming, no going,
No after, no before.
I hold you close,
I release you to be free;
I am in you
And you are in me.

No coming, no going is the true nature of reality. You have come from nowhere; you will go nowhere. The rose, the cloud, the mountains, the stars, the planet Earth—everything is like that. Their nature is the nature of no coming, no going. To die does not mean that from something you become nothing. To be born does not mean that from no one you suddenly become someone. There is only manifestation based on sufficient conditions, and the cessation of manifestation, based on the lack of proper conditions.

The sheet of paper on which these words are written has a history. This page in the book that you are holding in your hands took its form in a single moment. That does not mean that it was the moment of its birth. It was already there as the light of the sun, as the trunk of a tree, as the cloud and the earth. The moment when it came from the factory was just its moment of manifestation.

So we should ask, "Dear little sheet of paper, were you there before you were born?" The sheet of paper will answer, "Yes, in the form of a tree, in the form of the sunshine, in the form of a cloud and the rain, in the form of minerals and the earth. The moment of becoming a sheet of paper was a moment of continuation. I have not come from nothing. I have come from the cosmos. I have been a tree, I have been a cloud, I have been sunshine, soil and so on."

Looking deeply into the sheet of paper, you can still see the trees, the cloud, and the sunshine. You do not have to go to the past. That is the advantage of being a meditator; you do not have to travel. You just sit there and look deeply, and you can see and recognize everything. The sheet of paper contains all the information about the cosmos, including information concerning the cloud, the sunshine, the trees, the earth. If you return one of these elements to its origin, the sheet of paper will no longer be there. If you returned the sunshine to the sun, there would be no forest, and no paper. That is why the sunshine is in the paper. When you touch the sheet of paper, you touch the sunshine, you touch the cloud, you touch the rain, you touch the earth, you touch the whole cosmos. One manifestation contains all.

If you run your fingers over the paper, you can feel the cloud in it. Without the rain, which comes from the cloud, there would be no paper. When you are running your fingers over the piece of paper, you are running your fingers over the trees in the forest. With our fingers we can touch the sun and all the minerals of the earth in the paper. All these conditions lie in the paper. When we can be in touch with the paper with our awakened understanding, we are in touch with the whole of existence.

When we practice looking deeply into this sheet of paper, we can see the forest. Without the forest there would be no tree, without the trees we cannot make paper. So this sheet of paper has not come from nothing; it has come from something like the trees. But the trees are not enough to make the sheet of paper. The sunshine nourishes the trees; the clouds water the trees; the soil, the minerals and a multitude of other phenomena help the sheet of paper to manifest. And then there has to be a logger who cuts the tree, and the deli worker that made the sandwich for the logger's lunch, and the people who formed the company that pays the loggers. These things do not exist outside the sheet of paper. They are one with the paper.

You may think, *How can I identify this sheet of paper with the forest? The forest is outside the paper.* If you remove the forest or the cloud from the sheet of paper, the sheet of paper will fly apart. If there were no clouds, and no rain from the clouds, how could trees grow? How could we make paper paste in order to produce a sheet of paper?

The sheet of paper has no birthday, and you have no birthday. You were there before you were born. The next time you celebrate your birthday, you might like to change the song to "Happy Continuation Day." If it is true that the birthday is a continuation day, then what you call the day of death is also a continuation day. If your practice is strong, at the moment of dying you will sing a song of happy continuation.

Try to Make Nothing

You can try to make a sheet of paper into nothing. Is it possible? Strike a match and burn it to see whether it becomes nothing, or whether it becomes something else. This is not just a theory—it is something we can prove. Breathe in and out as you strike the match. Witness the transformation of a sheet of paper. As you light the match, be aware that the flame does not need to be born. With the right conditions, it only has to manifest for us to see it. As you burn the paper, see the smoke. The heat is enough to burn your fingers. Where is the paper now?

When you burn a sheet of paper, it is no longer in the form of paper. If you follow it with your mindfulness, you will see that the sheet of paper continues in other forms. One of its forms will be smoke. The smoke from the piece of paper rises and will join one or two of the clouds already existing in the sky. It is now participating in a cloud, and we can wave good-bye to it. Good-bye piece of paper, see you again very soon. Tomorrow, next month, there will be rain and a drop of water can fall on your forehead. That drop of water is your sheet of paper.

Another form the paper takes on is ash. You can give the ash back to the soil. When it is returned to the soil, the earth becomes a continuation of the sheet of paper. Maybe next year you will see the continuation of the paper in a tiny flower or a blade of grass. That is the afterlife of a sheet of paper.

During the process of being burned, the piece of paper also became heat. That heat penetrates into our bodies, even if you are not very close to the flame. Now you carry the sheet of paper in you. The heat penetrates deeply into the cosmos. If you are a scientist and have very sophisticated instruments, you can measure the effects of that heat even in distant planets and stars. They then become a manifestation, a continuation of the little sheet of paper. We cannot know how far the sheet of paper will go.

Scientists say that if you clap your hands it may have an impact on a distant star. What is happening with us can affect a galaxy far away. And the galaxy far away can affect us. Everything is under the influence of everything else.

Nothing Is Lost

To meditate means to be invited on a journey of looking deeply in order to touch our true nature and to recognize that nothing is lost. Because of this we can overcome fear. Non-fear is the greatest gift of meditation. With it we can overcome grief and our sorrow.

Only nothing can come from nothing. Something cannot come from nothing and nothing cannot come from something. If something is already there, it does not need to be born. The moment of birth is only a moment of continuation. You can be perceived as a baby the day of your so-called birth and everyone thinks of you as now existing. But you already existed before that day.

To die in our notion of death means that from something you suddenly become nothing. From someone you suddenly become no one—that is a horrible idea and makes no sense. If something has not been born, will that something have to die sometime? Can you reduce the sheet of paper into non-being, nothing?

I can testify that a sheet of paper has never been born, because to be born means from nothing you suddenly become something, from no one you suddenly become someone. That idea is not compatible with reality. Your true nature is the nature of no birth; the nature of the sheet of paper is also the nature of no birth. You have never been born; you have been there for a long, long time.

You Have Always Been There

When you were a child you may have liked to play with a kaleidoscope. Every movement of your fingers created a wonderful pattern of colors. If you moved it a little bit, then what you see would change. It was also beautiful, but it would be different. You might say that the different patterns within the kaleidoscope were being born or dying, but as a child you did not mourn that kind of birth and death. Instead, you continued to delight in seeing different forms and colors.

If we are able to touch our ground of no birth and no death, we will have no fear. That is the base of our true happiness. As long as fear is still in you, your happiness cannot be perfect. The bodhisattva Avalokiteshvara has offered us the Heart Sutra. In that sutra we learn that reality is as it is, not conditioned by birth, death, coming, going, being, non-being, increasing, decreasing, being defiled or immaculate. We are full of all these notions, and we suffer because we are caught in these notions. Our true liberation is the liberation from notions.

When you come to a practice center, you hope to alleviate some of your suffering. You hope for some relief, but the greatest relief of all can be obtained only by touching your true nature, the nature of no birth and no death. That is the deepest teaching the Buddha offered to us.

No Creation

Look at the sunflower growing in the garden. The sunflower relies on so many elements in order to manifest itself. There is a cloud inside of the flower because if there were no cloud there would be no rain, and no sunflower could grow. There is the sunshine in the sunflower. We know that without sunshine nothing can grow; there would be no sunflower. We see the earth, we see the minerals, we see the farmer, we see the gardener, and we see time, space, ideas, the willingness to grow and many other elements. So, sunflowers depend on many conditions in order to manifest, not just one.

I like to use the word "manifestation" instead of "birth," and I also like to use it instead of "creation." In our minds, "to create" also means from nothing something is brought forth. The farmer who grows sunflowers does not create the sunflowers. If you look deeply, you see that the farmer is only one of the conditions that can bring sunflowers into being. There are seeds of sunflowers stored in the barn, there are fields outside where you can plant sunflowers, there are clouds in the sky to make rain, there are fertilizers, there is the sunshine to help the sunflower to grow. You, the farmer, are not really the creator of the sunflower. You are just one of the conditions. Without you the sunflowers cannot manifest. But the same is true of the other conditions. All are equally important to the manifestation of the sunflower.

When you come to Plum Village in the month of July, you will see many sunflowers on the surrounding hills. Hundreds of thousands of sunflowers all turn toward the east, smiling and bright. If you come in the month of May or April, the hills are bare. But when the farmers walk through their fields, they can already see the sunflowers. They know that the sunflowers have been planted, that every condition is sufficient. The farmers have sown the seeds; the soil has been prepared. Only one condition is missing—the warmth that will come in June and July.

It is not because something manifests that you can describe it as being. It is not because it has not manifested or has ceased its manifestation that you can call it non-being. "Being" and "non-being" cannot apply to reality. By looking deeply, you realize that reality is not subject to birth and death, to being and non-being.

When Paul Tillich said, "God is the ground of being," that being should not be confounded with the being that is opposed to non-being. You are invited to look deeply into the notion of being in order to be free from it.

Five

NEW
BEGINNINGS

Where was Jesus before he was born? Over the years I have asked many of my Christian friends this question. If we want to look into this question deeply, we must explore the life and the death of Jesus in terms of manifestation. Jesus Christ was not no one before his birth. It was not in Bethlehem that Jesus came into being. The event of the nativity was only an occasion of manifestation; Jesus did exist before the moment of so-called birth or nativity. So we should not really call it a birth. It's not really the nativity. It's really only a manifestation. By looking with the insight of manifestation, we have an opportunity to see deeply into the person of Jesus. We can discover the truth of his immortality. We can discover the truth of our own nature of no birth and no death.

It is said by Christians that God sent his only son, Jesus, to earth. Since God was there, and Jesus is a part of God, and Jesus is the Son of God, Jesus was already there. The day of Christ's birth, Christmas, is a manifestation day, not a nativity day. This day was only the time when the manifestation took place.

Jesus Christ is still manifesting himself in many thousands of ways. He is manifesting himself all around you. We need to be alert in order to recognize his manifestations. If you are not mindful or attentive, you will miss him because you will miss his manifestations. In the morning when you practice walking meditation, you may recognize his manifestation as a flower, as a drop of water, as a bird song or as a child playing in the grass. We have to be very careful not to miss these things.

In the teaching and understanding of the Buddha, we all share the nature of no birth and no death. Not only humans, but also animals, plants and minerals share the nature of no birth and no death. A leaf and a flower share the same ground of no birth and no death. There is a manifestation of a flower or a leaf or a cloud. During the winter we do not see any sunflowers or dragonflies, and we do not hear the cuckoo bird sing. It seems that they do not exist in winter, but we know that this idea is wrong. In the beginning of spring, all of these beings will manifest themselves again. They have just been somewhere else during the winter, in another manifestation, waiting until conditions are favorable in order to manifest themselves again. To qualify them as non-existing in winter is a wrong perception.

NEW BEGINNINGS

"Passed Away" Does Not Mean "Gone"

We must also ask the question, If Jesus was not born then how could he die? Though he was crucified, did he cease to exist? And did Jesus need to be resurrected?

Is it possible that his crucifixion was not a death? Is it possible it was a hiding? His true nature is the nature of no birth and no death. This is true not just of Jesus. In this sense a cloud is the same, a sunflower is the same, and you and I are the same. We are not born and we do not die. And since Jesus Christ is not affected by birth and death, we call him the Living Christ.

It is real and deep wisdom to learn to look at things in terms of manifestation. If someone who is very close to you has passed away and you define him or her as non-existing, you are mistaken. From nothing cannot be born something. From no one cannot be born someone. From something you cannot become nothing. From someone you cannot become no one. That is the truth. If the person who is close to you does not manifest in the form that you are used to seeing or perceiving, that does not mean that he is non-existing. It does not mean that he is no longer there. If you look deeply, you can touch his or her presence in other forms of manifestation.

One day I took the hand of a young father who had just buried his little son. I invited him to walk with me to discover his son in other forms.

His son had come to Plum Village when he was very young and learned to enjoy vegetarian food. He gave me his allowance and extra pocket money and asked me to buy a plum tree and plant it for him. He wanted to participate in the work of supporting hungry children in the world by planting a fruit tree in Plum Village. He knew that a plum tree gives a lot of fruit. He knew that we could sell the fruit and send the money to hungry children in the third world. He learned to do walking and sitting meditation, and he practiced the dharma very well. When he was sick I went to Bordeaux and visited him in the hospital. He said to me, "Grandpa monk, I will do walking meditation for you." He got down from his bed, although he was quite weak, and walked beautifully for me. Shortly after my visit, he died. The day of his cremation, I sprinkled the consecrated water and chanted the Heart Sutra for him. A week later I took the hand of his father during a walking meditation and showed him many other manifestations of his little boy. Together we visited the plum tree I planted for his son, and as we sat in the afternoon light, we saw his little boy waving to us from every bud and branch.

Looking deeply into reality, you can discover many things. You can surmount so much suffering and counter many wrong perceptions. If we can abide peacefully in the ultimate dimension, we will not drown in the ocean of suffering, grief, fear and despair.

Re-Manifesting Ourselves

In the ultimate dimension, we have never been born and we will never die. In the historical dimension, we live in forgetfulness and we are rarely truly alive. We live like dead people.

In Albert Camus' novel *The Stranger*, the main character, out of despair and rage, shoots and kills someone. He receives the death sentence for his crime. One day, while lying on the bed in his prison cell, he looks up at the square-shaped skylight over him. Suddenly he becomes aware of and deeply in touch with the blue sky above. He has never seen the sky in that way before. Camus called this a moment of consciousness, which is a moment of awareness or of mindfulness. For the condemned man, it was the first time in his life that he really came into touch with the sky and realized what a miracle it was.

From that moment on, he wants to maintain that kind of shining awareness. He believes this was the only kind of energy that can keep him alive. He has only three days left before his execution. He practices all alone in the prison to maintain that awareness, to keep his mindfulness alive. He vows to live every minute of the three days left to him fully and in mindfulness. On his final day a priest comes to visit him to perform the last rites. The condemned man does not want to waste his time of awareness in receiving the sacrament. At first he resists, but finally he opens the door for the priest to come in. When the priest departs, the prisoner remarks to himself that the priest lives like a dead person. He has seen no qualities of awareness or mindfulness in the priest.

If you live without awareness it is the same as being dead. You cannot call that kind of existence being alive. Many of us live like dead people because we live without awareness. We carry our dead bodies with us and circulate throughout the world. We are pulled into the past or we are pulled forward into the future or we are caught by our projects or our despair and anger. We are not truly alive; we are not inhabited by awareness of the miracle of being alive. Albert Camus never studied Buddhism, but in his novel he speaks about a core practice of Buddhism, the *"moment de conscience,"* the moment of deep awareness or awakening.

The practice of resurrection, or re-manifestation, is possible for all of us. Our practice is always to resurrect our selves, going back to the mind and the body with the help of mindful breathing and walking. This will produce our true presence in the here and the now. Then we can become alive again. We will be like dead people reborn. We are free from the past, we are free from the future, we are capable of establishing ourselves in the here and now. We are fully present in the here and now, and we are truly alive. That is the basic practice of Buddhism. Whether you eat or drink or breathe or walk or sit, you can practice resurrection. Always allow yourself to be established in the here and now—fully present, fully alive. That is the real practice of resurrection.

The Only Moment We Can Be Alive

I have arrived, I am home
In the here, In the now
I am solid, I am free
In the ultimate, I dwell

We cannot enjoy life if we spend a lot of time worrying about what happened yesterday and what will happen tomorrow. We worry about tomorrow because we are afraid. If we are afraid all the time, we cannot appreciate that we are alive and can be happy now.

In our daily life, we tend to believe that happiness is only possible in the future. We are always looking for better things, the right conditions to make us happy. We run away from what is happening right in front of us. We try to find things that make us feel more solid, more safe and secure. But we are afraid all the time of what the future will bring. We are afraid we'll lose our jobs, our possessions, the people around us whom we love. So we wait for the magical moment—sometime in the future—when everything will be as we like, as we want it to be.

But life is available only in the present moment. The Buddha said, "It is possible to live happily in the present moment. It is the only moment we have."

When you come back to the here and the now, you will recognize the many conditions of happiness that already exist. The practice of mindfulness is the practice of coming back to the here and the now to be in touch deeply with ourselves, with life. We have to train ourselves in order to do this. Even if we are very intelligent and we understand it right away, we still have to train ourselves to live this way. We have to train ourselves to recognize that the conditions for happiness are already here.

True Home

Our true home is in the here and the now. The past is already gone and the future is not yet here. "I have arrived, I am home, in the here, in the now." This is our practice.

You can recite this *gatha*, or poem, during walking meditation or sitting meditation. You can practice this poem when you drive to your office. You may not have arrived at your office, but even while driving you have already arrived at your true home, the present moment. And when you arrive at your office, this is also your true home. When you are in your office, you are also in the here and the now.

Just practicing the first line of the poem "I have arrived, I am home" can make you very happy. Whether you are sitting, whether you are walking, whether you are watering the vegetables in the garden, or whether you are feeding your child, it is always possible to practice "I have arrived, I am home." I am not running anymore; I have run all my life; now I am determined to stop and to really live my life.

What Are You Waiting For?

The French have a song called: *"Qu'est-ce qu'on Attend Pour Etre Heureux?"* (What are you waiting for to be happy?). When I practice breathing in and I say, "I have arrived," that is an achievement. Now I am fully present, one hundred percent alive. The present moment has become my true home.

When I breathe out I say, "I am home." If you do not feel you are home, you will continue to run. And you will continue to be afraid. But if you feel you are already home, then you do not need to run anymore. This is the secret of the practice. When we live in the present moment, it is possible to live in true happiness.

Appreciating Earth

For many years I have told this story. Suppose two astronauts go to the moon. When they arrive, they have an accident and find out that they have only enough oxygen for two days. There is no hope of someone coming from Earth in time to rescue them. They have only two days to live. If you asked them at that moment, "What is your deepest wish?" they would answer, "To be back home walking on the beautiful planet Earth." That would be enough for them; they would not want anything else. They would not want to be the head of a large corporation, a big celebrity or president of the United States. They would not want anything except to be back on Earth—to be walking on Earth, enjoying every step, listening to the sounds of nature and holding the hand of their beloved while contemplating the moon.

We should live every day like people who have just been rescued from the moon. We are on Earth now, and we need to enjoy walking on this precious, beautiful planet. The Zen master Lin Chi said, "The miracle is not to walk on water but to walk on the Earth." I cherish that teaching. I enjoy just walking, even in busy places like airports and railway stations. In walking like that, with each step caressing our Mother Earth, we can inspire other people to do the same. We can enjoy every minute of our lives.

Six

THE
ADDRESS OF
HAPPINESS

If you want to know where God, the Buddhas and all the great beings live, I can tell you. Here is their address: in the here and now. It has everything you need, including the zip code.

If you can breathe in and out and walk in the spirit of "I have arrived, I am home, in the here, in the now," then you will notice that you are becoming more solid and more free immediately. You have established yourself in the present moment, at your true address. Nothing can push you to run anymore, or make you so afraid. You are free from worrying about the past. You are not stuck, thinking about what has not happened yet and what you cannot control. You are free from guilt concerning the past and you are free from your worries about the future.

Only a free person can be a happy person. The amount of happiness that you have depends on the amount of freedom that you have in your heart. Freedom here is not political freedom. Freedom here is freedom from regret, freedom from fear, from anxiety and sorrow. "I have arrived, I am home, in the here, in the now."

"I am solid, I am free." This is what you feel, what you become, when you arrive in the here and now. You're not just telling yourself this—you will see it; you will feel it. And when you do, you will be at peace. You will experience nirvana, or the kingdom of God, or whatever you may like to call it. Even if you are not caught by a lot of worries, if you are not solid and free, how can you be happy? To cultivate solidity and freedom in the present moment is the greatest gift we can give ourselves.

Dwelling in the Ultimate

"In the ultimate I dwell." The ultimate is the foundation of our being, the ground of being. The ultimate, or God, or the divine, is not separate from us. We are in it all the time. It is not somewhere up there beyond the sky. But we have to live in our true home in order to dwell in the ultimate, in order to live in the ultimate.

It is like the wave and water. If we look into a wave, we see that a wave can have a beginning and an end. A wave can be high or low. A wave can be like other waves, or it can be different. But the wave is always made of water. Water is the foundation of the wave. A wave is a wave, but it is also water. The wave may have a beginning and an end, it may be big or small, but with water there is no beginning, no end, no up, no down, no this, no that. When the wave realizes and understands this, it is free from the fear of beginning and end, up and down, big and small, this and that.

In the historical dimension, we have time and space, and pairs of opposites: right and wrong, young and old, coming and going, pure and impure. We look forward to beginning and we are afraid of ending. But the ultimate dimension does not have any of these things. There is no beginning or end, no before or after. The ultimate is the ground that makes the historical dimension possible. It is the original, continuing source of being. It is nirvana. It is the kingdom of God.

Our foundation is nirvana, the ultimate reality. You can call it God or the kingdom of God. This is the water in which we live. You are a wave, but at the same time you are also water. You have a historical dimension and you also have an ultimate dimension. If we understand that our true nature is of no birth, no death, no coming, no going, then our fear will depart and our pain and suffering will vanish.

A wave does not have to die in order to become water. She is water right here and now. We also do not have to die in order to enter the kingdom of God. The kingdom of God is our very foundation here and now. Our deepest practice is to see and touch the ultimate dimension in ourselves every day, the reality of no birth and no death. Only this practice can remove our fear and suffering entirely. Rather than saying, "In the ultimate I dwell," you may like to say, "In the kingdom of God I dwell" or "In the Buddha land I dwell."

Releasing Sorrow

Suppose someone was able to transport you by jet to the kingdom of God or the Pure Land of the Buddha. When you arrived, how would you walk? In such a beautiful place, would you walk under pressure, running and anxious like we do so much of the time? Or would you enjoy every moment of being in paradise? In the kingdom of God, or the Pure Land, people are free and they enjoy every moment. So they do not walk like we do.

The Pure Land is not somewhere else; it is right here, in the present. It is in every cell of our bodies. When we run away from the present, we destroy the kingdom of God. But if we know how to free ourselves from our habit energy of running, then we will have peace and freedom and we will all walk like a Buddha in paradise.

What we carry with us determines in which dimension we dwell. If you carry a lot of sorrow, fear and craving with you, then wherever you go you will always touch the world of suffering and hell. If you carry with you compassion, understanding and freedom, then wherever you go you will touch the ultimate dimension, the kingdom of God.

Wherever the practitioner goes, she knows she is touching the kingdom of God under her feet. There is not one day when I do not walk in the kingdom of God. Because I practice freedom and compassion wherever I go, my feet touch the kingdom of God, the ultimate dimension everywhere. If we cultivate this kind of touching, then the important elements of solidity and freedom will be available to us twenty-four hours every day.

"I have arrived, I am home." The home of the wave is water. It's right there. She does not have to travel thousands of miles in order to arrive at her true home. It's so simple and so powerful. I would like to invite you to memorize this little poem and to practice and remember it many times a day. In this way you will touch the ultimate dimension and always remember your true home.

Habit Energy of Running

We run during the daytime and we run during our sleep. We do not know how to stop. Our practice is first of all to stop, then to relax, to calm down and to concentrate. When we can do this, then we are in the here and now. Then we become solid. And when we are solid, we can look around. We can look deeply into the present moment, we can look deeply into our true nature, and we can discover the ultimate dimension. By looking deeply, we can see that though we are waves, we are also water. But if we have not stopped, if we have not learned to concentrate, then we cannot look deeply. We will not free ourselves from fear because we will not be strong enough or stable enough to see the reality of no coming and no going.

It is very hard to fight against the habits we have developed. Dr. Ambedkar was a member of Indian parliament who came from the ranks of the Untouchables. He fought for the rights of the Untouchables. He felt very strongly that their hope for dignity and safety was in Buddhism. The Buddha did not believe in the caste system. So, one day in the city of Bombay, five hundred thousand Untouchables came together and Dr. Ambedkar delivered the Three Refuges and the Five Mindfulness Trainings of the Buddha. I went to India to offer my support and assistance to this community of Untouchables. We gave dharma talks and held days of mindfulness.

Imagine that you grew up as an Untouchable. Imagine that everyone around you treated you badly and made you afraid for your life. Imagine that you had to please all those of higher rank in order to stay safe. How would you live? Would you be relaxed and in the present moment? Or in constant worry about the future? The habit energy of anxiety would be very strong.

The friend who organized my trip came from the Untouchable community. He lived in New Delhi with his wife and three children. He very much wanted to make my trip pleasant and successful. One morning, we were sitting on a bus together, traveling to another community. I was enjoying the landscape of India from my window seat. When I turned to look at my friend, I noticed that he was very tense. I said, "My dear friend, I know that you very much want to make my trip pleasant and happy, but you know, I am very happy right now! Please, don't worry. Sit back and relax!" He said, "Yes!" He relaxed a bit, so I turned to the window again and I practiced breathing in and out. I enjoyed the palm trees in the morning sun.

I thought about the palm leaves on which the scriptures of the Buddha have been written since ancient times. The leaves are long and slender. A sharp point was used to inscribe the teaching of the Buddha on the leaves. They can be preserved for a thousand years or more. I remembered that some fifteen-hundred-year-old Buddhist texts had been discovered in Nepal written on these leaves. Then my mind returned to my friend. This took perhaps two minutes. I turned to him and saw that he was becoming stiff and tense again. It was difficult for him to relax for even a few minutes.

As an Untouchable, he had struggled all of his life. Now,

even though he had a nice apartment in New Delhi and a good job, the habit energy in him to struggle all the time was still very strong. Throughout many generations, the Untouchables have been struggling hard day and night to survive. That kind of habit energy had been transmitted to him from many generations. It would be difficult for anyone to transform it quickly. He needed some time and some training. With the support of friends in the practice, in a few months or a few years he could transform his energy of struggling and being tense. It is possible for anyone to do. You can allow yourself to relax and be free.

If you want to transform your habit energy of running and struggling, you have to recognize it every time it shows its head. Breathing in and out and smiling, you say, "Oh, my dear little habit energy, I know you are there!" At that moment you are free. You can remind yourself. You can teach yourself. You cannot have a spiritual friend twenty-four hours a day with you to remind you. I reminded my friend one time, and it worked only for two minutes. He has to do it himself. Everyone has to do it for themselves. You must become your own spiritual friend and live in an environment that helps you.

The habit energy of running is strong in us. It may have been transmitted to us by many generations. But you don't need to pass that habit energy along. You should be able to tell your children that you have walked in the kingdom of

God. You may like to tell them, as I have told my friends, that there is not one day when I do not walk in the kingdom of God. If you can do this, your life will become an inspiration to many people. Perhaps you and your children will walk in the Pure Land all the time.

Releasing Our Baggage

If we want to walk in the Pure Land all the time, it helps us to let go of the things that keep us from being in the present. It helps us to learn to let go of what makes us worry, to get to zero. When we think of zero, we think of it as nothingness. We see it as something negative. But zero can be very positive. If you have a debt to pay, that is negative. When you pay it back, your balance returns to zero. That is wonderful because then you are free.

At the time of the Buddha, there was a monk whose name was Baddhiya. Before becoming a monk he had been governor of a province in the kingdom of Sakka where the Buddha was born. After his enlightenment the Buddha had come back to the kingdom of his birth and visited his family. When many young people saw the great happiness and liberty of the Buddha, they wanted to follow him. They wanted to be free.

Among them was Baddhiya. During the first three months

of his monastic life he practiced so diligently that he could see many things deeply. One night while practicing meditation in the forest, he opened his mouth and said, "Oh my happiness! Oh my happiness!"

As governor, Baddhiya had slept in beautiful rooms. He was guarded by many soldiers. He had expensive things to eat and many servants. Now he sat at the foot of a tree, with nothing but his begging bowl and monk's robe.

A monk who was sitting close to Baddhiya heard his exclamation. He thought Baddhiya regretted losing his former positions of power. He thought Baddhiya must be regretting losing his former life as a governor. In the early morning of the next day the monk went to the Buddha and told him what he had heard. The Buddha summoned Baddhiya and in the presence of the entire community of monks the Buddha said, "Brother Baddhiya, is it true that last night during sitting meditation you opened your mouth and pronounced the words, "Oh my happiness! Oh my happiness?" Baddhiya replied, "Yes, that is true, Lord Buddha."

The Buddha asked, "Why? Did you regret something?"

Baddhiya answered, "During sitting meditation, I remembered the time when I was governor, attended by so many servants and protected by bodyguards. I always lay awake with fear. I was afraid that people would steal my wealth from me. I was afraid of being assassinated. Now, sitting at the foot of a tree and meditating, I felt so free. Now I have nothing to lose. I enjoy deeply every moment, and I have never been as happy as I am now. That is why I said, 'Oh my happiness! Oh my happiness!' Noble Teacher, if I disturbed my brothers, I apologize." Only then did everyone in the sangha understand that Baddhiya's words were an expression of his real happiness.

Please take a pen and a sheet of paper. Go to the foot of a tree or to your writing desk, and make a list of all the things that can make you happy right now: the clouds in the sky, the flowers in the garden, the children playing, the fact that you have met the practice of mindfulness, your beloved ones sitting in the next room, your two eyes in good condition. The list is endless. You have enough already to be happy now. You have enough to be free from coming and going, up and down, birth and death. Nourish yourself every day with the wonderful things that life has to offer you. Nourish yourself in the present moment. Walk in the kingdom of God.

What Are We Running After?

If we are not fully present and not alive, either for our loved ones or ourselves, where are we? We are running, running, running, even during our sleep. We run because our fear of losing everything is chasing us. The practice of resurrection can help us.

When you come back to mindfulness and awareness, when the energy of mindfulness is present in you, the energy of the Holy Spirit is present in you. The Holy Spirit makes life possible. To be inhabited by the Holy Spirit is our practice. To live every moment in the presence of the Holy Spirit is not something abstract. It can be done when you drink your juice or your tea. Drink in such a way that the Holy Spirit is present in you. When you eat some muesli, some rice or some tofu, eat it in such a way that the Holy Spirit is present in you. When you walk you should allow the Holy Spirit to be walking in you.

Please do not practice only for the sake of form. Every walking meditation session is a new walking meditation session. Walk in such a way that you will be nourished with every step you make. Every meal should be a new meal where you can nourish yourself with the energy of the Holy Spirit, the energy of mindfulness. Every sitting session should be a new sitting session.

Sit in such a way that allows your new being to manifest. Let us practice with friends. The sangha is intelligent enough, is smart enough not to fall into the trap of doing the practice as a routine and not as something creative. Many of us are intelligent and creative. We should use our intelligence and our creativity in order to keep the practice alive and constantly renewed. It is perfectly possible to practice this kind of Buddhist meditation as a Christian, as a Muslim, as a Hindu or as a Jew. It doesn't matter what religion you practice, or even if you practice no religion at all.

To practice does not mean to imitate the form. To practice means to use our intelligence and our skills to make nourishment and transformation possible in our self, engendering nourishment and transformation in the people around us.

New Beginnings

When you eat your bread or your croissant in the morning, eat in such a way that the bread becomes life. Celebrate the Eucharist every morning while breaking the bread or biting into your croissant. Feel alive; feel that you are in touch with the whole cosmos. If the piece of bread is the body of Jesus, it is also the body of the cosmos. "This piece of bread is the body of the cosmos," we can say. Eating with mindfulness allows you to recognize the piece of bread as the body of the cosmos. When you eat like this, you are a new person. Allow the new being to manifest in you. You can do this practice by yourself. You can also practice this with others in order to help your brothers and sisters renew themselves every moment of their daily practice.

When we begin the practice, we have the gift of beginner's mind. Beginner's mind is a beautiful mind. You are motivated by the desire to practice, to transform yourself, to bring peace and joy into yourself, and that peace and joy becomes contagious. Allow yourself to be a torch, and allow the flame of your torch to be transmitted to other torches. Practicing like that, you can help peace and joy grow in the entire world.

The practice of resurrection should be taken up by each of us. When we practice it with success we will also help other people around us. This is the true practice of being alive. Whatever we do in our daily practice—walking, sitting, eating or sweeping the floor—the purpose of all these things is to help us become alive again. Be alive in every moment, and by waking up yourself, you will wake up the world.

Waking up is the very nature of the teaching and the practice. "Budh" means to wake up. We call the one who is awake a Buddha. The Buddha is someone who dispenses the teachings and the practice of awakening. Each of us can transform his- or herself into a lamp that can help the entire world awaken.

Seven

CONTINUING
MANIFESTATIONS

The Buddha has advised us that we should not accept any teachings as true just because a famous master teaches them or because they are found in holy books. This also includes the Buddhist canon. We can only accept teachings that we have put into practice with our own awakened understanding and that we can see with our own experience to be true. The Buddha said our true nature is the nature of no birth and no death. Let us look again and see if this is true.

If you light a candle and the flame keeps burning until the whole candle is finished, is the candle still there or not? The Buddha says there is no annihilation. We have seen that this is true. And also we have seen that the concept of permanence is not applicable to things as they are. So the truth lies somewhere in between. Here, we must look deeply with all our concentration.

Do you think that the flame on the candle is going down only in a vertical direction? If you think so, then you are following the flame in time. You may also think in this way about your own life span: that it is going in a linear direction and that one day it will end. You may think that you were born on a point on a vertical line, a point you may call 1960. You may think that you will die on a point somewhere farther down on that line, which you may call 2040. All you can see is yourself moving in time like the candle. But you are not just moving in a linear direction.

You might think that the flame is just going down. You might think that the candle will die. In fact the flame is going out in many other directions. It is giving out light all around itself to the north, south, east and west. If you had a very sensitive scientific instrument, you would be able to measure the heat and light that the candle is sending out into the universe. The candle is going into you as an image, as light and as heat.

You are like a candle. Imagine you are sending light out around you. All your words, thoughts and actions are going in many directions. If you say something kind, your kind words go in many directions, and you yourself go with them.

We are transforming and continuing in a different form at every moment. This morning you said something unkind to your child. With those unkind words you went into her heart. Now you are regretting what you said. It does not mean that you cannot transform what you have said by admitting your mistake to your child, but if you fail to do so, those unkind words may stay with your child for a long time.

Three Dimensions

Now I am writing a dharma book. It is made of my understanding and my practice. When I write a dharma book, I am not going in a linear direction. I am going out into you, and I am being reborn in different forms in you. In Buddhism we talk of the three actions, the three dimensions—the dimensions of body, speech and mind—at every moment of our lives. Try to see this and understand this truth; you do not need to wait until your body disintegrates to go on the journey of rebirth.

At this very moment we are being born and we are dying. We are being reborn not in one single form but in many forms. I would like you to imagine a firecracker. When you light a firework it does not go down in a vertical direction. It goes out in many dimensions, and the sparks go out in all directions. So do not think that you go in only one direction. You are like fireworks. You go out into your children, your friends, your society and the whole world.

In the morning when I do sitting meditation, to my left and to my right are monks. I have been reborn in them by sitting with them. If you look carefully you will see me in them. I am not waiting to be reborn after I die. I am being reborn in this moment, and I want to be reborn in a good direction. I want to hand on to my lay and monastic friends the most beautiful and happy things of my life so that they can have a good rebirth for me and for themselves.

Our ignorance, anger and despair should not be reborn. When they are reborn they bring more darkness and suffering into the world. The more happiness and love that can be reborn the better, because it will make this world more beautiful and kind. Therefore you and I should be living our weeks, days and hours in order to be reborn constantly as happiness, love and kindness.

One day as I woke up I remembered the words of a folk song, "My father and mother have given me much merit." Their merit is my generosity, love, forgiveness and capacity to offer joy and happiness to others. They have given me this precious inheritance. Our children are our continuation. We are our children and our children are us. If you have one or more children, you have already been reborn in them. You can see your continuation body in your son or your daughter, but you have many more continuation bodies as well. They are in everyone you have touched. And you cannot know how many people your words, actions and thoughts have touched.

Giving Our Heat and Light

When the flame of the candle has given its light and its heat all around it, that light and heat are the continuation of the candle. That light and heat go out in a horizontal plane. In order to give the light and heat in a horizontal plane, it must also burn in a vertical direction. Without the horizontal dimension, there cannot be a vertical dimension. And without the vertical dimension, there can be no horizontal dimension.

Ask yourself, "Where shall I go after this?" Our actions and our words, which are being produced at this moment, take us in a linear direction. But they also take us in a lateral direction as they flow into and influence the world around us. They can make the world more beautiful and bright. That beauty and brightness can go into the future. We should not look for our real selves in just one vertical direction.

When I make a pot of oolong tea, I put tea leaves into the pot and pour boiling water on them. Five minutes later there is tea to drink. When I drink it, oolong tea is going into me. If I put in more hot water, making a second pot of tea, the tea from those leaves continues to go into me. After I have poured out all the tea, what will be left in the pot is just the spent tea leaves. The leaves that remain are only a very small part of the tea. The tea that goes into me is a much bigger part of the tea. It is the richest part.

We are the same; our essence has gone into our children, our friends and the entire universe. We have to find ourselves in those directions and not in the spent tea leaves. I invite you to see yourself reborn in forms that you say are not yourself. You have to see your body in what is not your body. This is called your body outside of your body.

You do not have to wait until the flame has gone out to be reborn. I am reborn many times every day. Every moment is a moment of rebirth. My practice is to be reborn in such a way that my new forms of manifestation will bring light, freedom and happiness into the world. My practice is not to allow wrong actions to be reborn. If I have a cruel thought or if my words carry hatred in them, then those thoughts and words will be reborn. It will be difficult to catch them and pull them back. They are like a runaway horse. We should try not to allow our actions of body, speech and mind to take us in the direction of wrong action, wrong speech and wrong thinking.

Living Through Birth and Death

If there were not birth and death in every moment, we could not continue to live. In every moment, many cells in your body have to die so that you can continue to live. Not only the cells of your body but all the feelings, perceptions and mental formations in the river of consciousness in you are born and die in every moment.

I remember the day a friend brought the ashes of his father, who had been cremated, to the Upper Hamlet of Plum Village. He asked to be allowed to sprinkle this ash by the walking meditation path, and I agreed. He may have thought that the only thing his father had left behind on the walking meditation path was his ash. But when his father was alive, he had walked on that path where his ashes were now sprinkled. We performed the ceremony of sprinkling the ashes. Afterward, I turned to the group and said, "Each of us has left our body on this walking meditation path, not only this person who has died, but each of us. Every time we practice walking on this path we leave behind cells from our body."

Whenever you scratch yourself, thousands of dead skin cells fall to the ground. When you walk on the meditation path, you not only leave behind the skin cells of your body, you also leave behind your feelings, perceptions and mental formations. Whether you spend an hour or a week in Plum Village, after you have gone, you leave behind many traces of yourself. The cells that you leave behind on the path become grass and wild flowers. Your continuation body is still there in Plum Village. It is in your children and grandchildren also. It is in every part of the world. When the flame of the candle reaches the end of the wick and goes out, it is still there. You cannot find it by looking only in a linear direction. You have to find it also in the horizontal direction.

In the Tibetan tradition, whenever a high lama dies, fellow

monks wait a few years and then go and look for the continuation body of that person. The continuation is called a *tulku* in
Tibetan. The high lama may have left a poem toward the end
of this life, which is thought to contain clues about where his
continuation body might be found. Using this poem, his disciples go looking for a young child who would be a suitable
candidate. They go to the house of that child, bringing with
them some instruments such as a bell, rosary or teacup that
their teacher had used. They mix them in with similar items
that he had not used. The young child has to pick out from
this assortment the instruments of the high lama who has
passed away. If he does this, then, after passing other exami-
nations, he is proclaimed as the continuation of the deceased
teacher. The monastic disciples of the former high lama ask
the parents to give permission to take the child to the
monastery so that he can continue to be their teacher for the
next generation.

There is something very appealing about this tradition.
The disciples have so much love and respect for their teacher
that they want to keep their teacher with them after he has
passed away. I have often said to my friends in Plum Village
that they should not wait for me to pass away in order to
look for my continuation body. They have to look for me
now because I have already been reborn in many young children. If you were standing with me now, would you see my
spiritual children beside me? They are all my continuation. I

have hundreds of thousands of continuations in young people who continue the practice of mindfulness. If you look with dharma eyes, you will see me reborn in many forms.

Although my books and my dharma talks are not allowed to be published in Vietnam, I am there. My teachings are still circulated widely, although they are not legally allowed. The security police confiscate my books and secretly read them. Others print and publish them underground. So I continue in Vietnam. There are young monks and nuns in Vietnam who are practicing the dharma doors that I teach. If you go to Vietnam you will see me there. The body that you see here is just one manifestation of myself. My presence in Vietnam influences the spiritual life, the culture and the young people of Vietnam. Someone who says I am not in Vietnam does not have dharma eyes.

I have taught in prisons, and my books have been distributed in correctional facilities throughout the United States. Many prisoners have read and enjoyed them. One time I was able to visit a maximum-security prison in Maryland. It was so strict that not even an ant could find its way in without being stopped. I taught the prisoners on the subject of being free wherever you are. This teaching has been transcribed and published as a book.* Many copies have been given to prisons so that prisoners can practice and smile,

* *Be Free Where You Are* by Thich Nhat Hanh, published by Parallax Press.

and can suffer less. They manage to find real joy even in prison life, so I know that I am now in prison. Those prisoners who have practiced help other prisoners. All the prisoners who come into touch with my teachings are my continuation body. When you look for me, do not look at this body. Look outside this body.

Fireworks

If you learn to see yourself every day going out in a lateral direction and being reborn at every moment, you will be able to find yourself in the future by looking in that lateral dimension. You are just like a firework going off in every moment. The firework diffuses its beauty around itself. With your thoughts, words and actions you can diffuse your beauty. That beauty and goodness goes into your friends, into your children and grandchildren and into the world. It is not lost, and you go into the future in that way.

If you look for yourself like that, you will be able to see your continuation in the future. You will not be caught in the idea that you will be annihilated. You will not be caught in the notion that you will not exist anymore when you die. The truth is that you are not permanent, but neither are you annihilated.

Can you see yourself being reborn every moment of the

past? All your ancestors continue in you, and when you transform the habit energies that they have transmitted to you, you are being reborn in the past. For instance, maybe your ancestors had the habit of always running, needing to be working or doing something to survive. They did not have the time to stop, breathe and be in touch with the wonderful things that life has to offer. You, too, used to be like that, but you have now met the practice. Now you can stop, you can breathe and be in touch with the wonderful things of life for your ancestors. Maybe your genetic or spiritual ancestors had beautiful traits that your parents or the spiritual teachers you met during your life have failed to manifest fully. Now you can rediscover those things in yourself, and you can revive what seemed to have been lost. That is also being reborn in the past.

There was an American Vietnam veteran I knew. The guerrillas had killed his comrades, and he was determined to take revenge on the people of the village where his comrades had died. He made sandwiches of bread with explosives in the filling and left them at the entrance of the village. Some children came and found the sandwiches and began to eat them. Soon they were writhing and howling in pain. Their parents ran to the scene, but it was too late. The area was remote, without ambulances and medical equipment, and the children could not be brought to the hospital quickly enough. All five of them died.

After he returned to the United States, the soldier could not overcome his guilt. His mother tried to comfort him. She said, "My son, those things happen in war. There is nothing to feel bad about." But still, he suffered so much. Whenever he found himself in a room with children, he could not bear it. He had to run out.

During one of my tours in the United States, a retreat was organized for war veterans. I taught them how to walk and breathe in order to transform their fear, guilt and suffering. I said to this veteran, "You have killed five children; that is true. But you can save the lives of hundreds of children. Do you know that every day, tens of thousands of children die for want of food and medicine? You can bring food and medicine to some of them." He practiced as I advised, and that person who, twenty years ago, had killed five children was immediately reborn in the past as someone who saved the lives of twenty children.

Learn to look deeply like this, and your regrets and your lack of confidence will be transformed. You will have new energy, which will not only sparkle in the past but will also shine in the present and the future.

Eight

FEAR, ACCEPTANCE AND FORGIVENESS: THE PRACTICE OF TOUCHING THE EARTH

Many of us spend a lot of time asking the question: "Why do I have to die?" The more important question to ask ourselves is: "What happens before I die?" You must go to your beloved one and ask: "Darling, who are you? Are you the same person as the one I married thirty years ago or are you different? Why have you come here? Where will you go? Why shall I have to weep one day when you die?" These are very important questions that cannot be answered by our intellect alone. We need something deeper and more complete.

The practice of Touching the Earth can help us touch our true nature of no birth and no death. If we practice Touching the Earth as the Buddha practiced, it can help us to achieve real insight.

It is written in the sutras that the day before Prince Siddhartha became the Buddha, the Enlightened One, he had a little doubt about his ability to become fully awake. He had been quite confident, but then something made him question it. So he practiced Touching the Earth. He used his hand to touch the earth in order to transform that doubt. The next day, Prince Siddhartha became Buddha.

In Buddhist temples throughout Asia, you will see statues of the Buddha touching the Earth with his hand. Touching the Earth is a very deep practice that can help us transform our fears, doubts, prejudice and anger.

Touching Both Dimensions

The historical dimension and the ultimate dimension of reality are related to each other. If you can deeply touch one, you can touch the other. Jesus Christ can be referred to as both the Son of Man and the Son of God. As Son of Man, he belongs to the historical dimension. As Son of God, he belongs to the ultimate dimension.

There is the historical Buddha but there is also the Buddha who is not limited by space and time. We are all like that. We have a historical dimension, which we live every day, but we also have an ultimate dimension, which we try to live using our spiritual practice. If we can live in the ultimate dimension at the same time as we function in the historical, we will have no more fear. When there is no more fear, there is true happiness. A wave has a right to live her life as a wave, but she must also learn to live her life as water because she is not only a wave. She is also water. And water lives without the fear carried by the wave.

Touching the Earth is an easy and effective way to touch our ultimate dimension. If you do this practice, one day you will touch your true nature of no birth and no death. At that time, you will be liberated from fear. You can become someone who rides majestically on the waves of birth and death because you are no longer agitated by fear or anger.

Touching the Earth:
The Historical Dimension

Imagine the dimension of time as a vertical line. Place yourself standing in the present on that line with the past above you and the future below you. Establish yourself in time. See all your ancestors that have come before you. The youngest generation of your ancestors is your parents. All of them are above you on this line of time. Then below you, see all your descendants, your children, your grandchildren and all their future generations. If you have no children, your descendants are the people you have touched in your life, and all the people they in turn influence.

In you are both your blood ancestors and your spiritual ancestors. You touch the presence of your father and mother in each cell of your body. They are truly present in you, along with your grandparents and great-grandparents. Doing this, you realize you are their continuation. You may have thought that your ancestors no longer existed, but even scientists will say that they are present in you, in your genetic heritage, which is in every cell of your body.

The same is true for your descendants. You will be present in every cell of their bodies. And you are present in the consciousness of everyone you have touched. This is real, not imagined.

This is the first touching of the earth.

Pits and Trees

Look into a plum tree. In each plum on the tree there is a pit. That pit contains the plum tree and all previous generations of plum tree. The plum pit contains an eternity of plum trees. Inside the pit is an intelligence and wisdom that knows how to become a plum tree, how to produce branches, leaves, flowers and plums. It cannot do this on its own. It can only do this because it has received the experience and heritage of so many generations of ancestors. You are the same. You possess the wisdom and intelligence of how to become a full human being because you inherited an eternity of wisdom not only from your blood ancestors but from your spiritual ancestors, too.

Your spiritual ancestors are in you because what you are

by nature and what you are by nurture cannot be separated. Nurturing transforms your inherited nature. Your spirituality and your practice, which are parts of your daily life, are also in every cell of your body. So your spiritual ancestors are in every cell of your body. You cannot deny their presence.

You have ancestors whom you admire and of whom you are proud. You also have ancestors who had many negative traits and of whom you are not proud, but they are still your ancestors. Some of us have wonderful parents; others have parents who suffered a lot and made their spouses and their children suffer. Or you may have had spiritual ancestors who did not help you to appreciate the religion practiced by your family and your community. You may not have respect for them now, but they are still your ancestors.

Acceptance

We need to return to ourselves and embrace our blood and our spiritual ancestors. We cannot get rid of them. They are a fact and they are there. They are part of our bodies and our souls.

When you touch the earth the first time, practice accepting all your ancestors just as they are. This is very important. Unconditional acceptance is the first step in opening the door to the miracle of forgiveness. Jesus said, "Forgive us our trespasses as we forgive those who have trespassed against us." He understood that the first step of forgiveness is to accept other people just as they are, even if they have harmed us.

To accept others as they are, we must begin with ourselves. If we cannot accept ourselves as we are, we will never be able to accept others. When I look at myself, I see positive, admirable and even remarkable things, but I also know that there are negative parts of me. So first I recognize and accept myself.

Wherever you are standing to practice Touching the Earth—before a rock, or mountain, or flower or altar in your home—practice conscious breathing. Breathing in and breathing out, you visualize your ancestors, and you see all their positive and negative points. Be determined to accept them all as your ancestors without hesitation. After that, you prostrate, touching the earth with your knees, your hands and your forehead. Stay in that position while you continue the visualization:

"Dear ancestors, I am you, with all your strengths and weaknesses. I see you have negative and positive seeds. I understand that you have been lucky and that good seeds like kindness, compassion and fearlessness were watered in you. I also understand that if you were not lucky and negative seeds like greed, jealousy and fear were watered in you, then the positive seeds did not have a chance to grow."

If positive seeds are watered in a person's life, it is partly because of luck and partly because of effort. The circumstances of our lives can help us water the seeds of patience, generosity, compassion and love. The people around us can help us water these seeds, and so can the practice of mindfulness.

But if a person grew up in a time of war, or in a family and community with great suffering, then that person may be full of despair and fear. If they had parents who had suffered a lot and were afraid of the world and other people, then they would transmit this fear and anger to their children. If they grew up embraced by security and love, the good seeds nurtured in them would grow, and these wonderful seeds would be transmitted.

If you can look like that at your ancestors, you will understand that they are human beings who have suffered and have tried their best. That understanding will remove all rejection and anger. It is very important to be able to accept all your ancestors with both their strengths and weaknesses. It will help you to become more peaceful and less afraid.

You can also see your elder brothers and sisters as your very young ancestors because they were born before you. They too have weaknesses as well as talents, which you have to accept because you realize that you yourself have weaknesses and talents. This kind of acceptance is what you realize as you touch the earth. If you need to, you can maintain the prostrate position for five, ten or fifteen minutes to look deeply and realize this acceptance.

The first Touching of the Earth may have to be repeated several times before you can become reconciled with your parents and your ancestors. It takes a lot of practice, but it is important to do because, since your parents and your ancestors are in you, to reconcile with them is to reconcile with yourself. To deny your ancestors is to deny yourself. If you can see that you are not separate from your ancestors, that is great progress. I am sure you can be successful after a few days or a week of this practice.

You can do the practice of Touching the Earth anywhere, before your ancestral altar, before a tree, a cloud, a mountain or anywhere else you like. Standing before a rock or a cloud or a tree or a flower on your altar, visualize the presence of all your ancestors in you. It is not difficult, because you are in fact them. You are their continuation. Please practice with one hundred percent of your being.

Touching the Future

The next step in the practice of Touching the Earth is to look at your descendants—your children, grandchildren, nieces and nephews. If you have difficulties with them you should visualize as follows:

"I am not an entity separate from my children, because I

am continued by my children. They carry me into the future. My son, daughter, friend or disciple is me."

In the obituary notices they always write, "Mister X has died and is survived by his sons and daughters." The idea here is that the children continue to live for the father. My disciples are me and I live every day in such a way as to be able to transmit the best of myself to them because they are going to carry me into the future. I have told my disciples that they should watch the sunrise for me and I will watch the sunset and the stars for them with their eyes. I am immortal because of my disciples.

Just as you see yourself in your parents and your ancestors, so you can see yourself in your son and daughter. Thanks to your parents you have access to your source in all your ancestors. My disciples have access to the Buddha and ancestral teachers through me. Thanks to your children you have access to the future. The son needs his father to have access to his source, and the father needs his son to have access to the future and the infinite.

This is a very concrete practice that you can do alone or with one or two friends for mutual support. In the beginning someone can help you by guiding your practice as you do it. But later on you can guide yourself.

Trying to Separate

If you have difficulties with your son or daughter, you may have the tendency to say: "You are not my daughter. *My* daughter would not behave like that" or "You are not my son. *My* son would never do things like that." If you look deeply at yourself, you will see that these negative seeds are in you also. When you were young you made mistakes and you learned from your suffering. When your child makes mistakes, you need to help him understand so he will not do it again. When you can see your own weaknesses, you can say: "Who am I not to accept my son?" Your son is you. With this insight into non-duality, you can reconcile with your children. The practice of Touching the Earth is a path to reconciliation.

Right Concentration

The Noble Eightfold Path, the path of the eight right practices taught by the Buddha, has as its last component Right Concentration. The concentration on no self, impermanence and interconnectedness is what we realize when we touch the earth. Without this concentration there will be no insight. If you can see yourself, your parents and your children in the light of impermanence, no self and interconnectedness, then reconciliation will come very naturally.

Give yourself time to practice Touching the Earth once a day or even twice. You can use the following words to guide your visualization: "Touching the earth, I connect with my ancestors and all descendants of my spiritual and blood families." (*Visualize this for a short time standing before your preferred object, and then touch the earth*).

My spiritual ancestors include the Buddha, the bodhisattvas and the Buddha's disciples. They include my own spiritual teachers, those still alive and those who have already passed away. They are present in me because they have transmitted to me seeds of peace, wisdom, love and happiness. They have woken up in me my own resource of understanding and compassion. When I look at my spiritual ancestors, I see those who are perfect in the practice of the mindfulness trainings, understanding and compassion, and those who are imperfect. I accept them all because I see within myself shortcomings and weaknesses also.

Aware that my practice of the mindfulness trainings is not always perfect, and that I am not always understanding and compassionate, I open my heart and accept all my spiritual descendants. Some of my descendants live in such a way as to invite my confidence and respect, but there are those who have many difficulties and are subject to ups and downs in their practice. I open my heart and embrace them all equally.

In the same way, I accept all my ancestors on my mother's side and my father's side of the family. I accept all their good qualities, all the virtuous things they have done, and I also accept all their weaknesses. I open my heart and accept all my blood descendants with their good qualities, their talents and also their weaknesses.

Whatever tradition your spiritual roots are in, you can include teachers from that tradition. If you have Christian roots your spiritual ancestors include Christ, Christ's disciples, the saints and the Christian teachers who have touched your life. If you have Jewish roots you may want to include the patriarchs and matriarchs and the great rabbis.

My spiritual ancestors, blood ancestors, spiritual descendants and blood descendants are all part of me. I am they and they are me. I do not have a separate self. We all exist as part of a wonderful stream of life.

Meditation on the Historical Dimension

The historical dimension is the dimension of coming and going, birth and death. When we begin to touch the historical dimension, often we can become afraid. We are afraid because we do not yet understand that birth and death are not real.

The Buddha said, "Anything that is born must die." If there is birth, then there must be death also. If the right is there the left must be there also. If there is a beginning, then there must be an end. That is the way things appear to be in the historical dimension. The monks, the nuns and the laypeople in the time of the Buddha practiced recognizing birth and death as realities.

In order to face our fear, it helps to stabilize the mind a little bit through meditation and contemplation. At first, it is easier to practice when we are guided. Breathing is the vehicle that carries concentration. It directs your mind to the object of your meditation. We begin through the awareness of breathing, so that later, when we need to contemplate, we will be able to direct the mind.

We try to direct the mind toward recognizing reality. This is a chant that is recited daily in Buddhist monasteries: "Breathing in and out, I am aware of the fact that I am of the nature to die; I cannot escape dying. I am of the nature to grow old; I cannot escape old age. I am of the nature to get sick. Because I have a body, I cannot avoid sickness. Everything I cherish, treasure and cling to today, I will have to abandon one day. The only thing I can carry with me is the fruit of my own action. I cannot bring along with me anything else except the fruit of my actions in terms of thought, speech and bodily acts."

We have to recognize this reality and smile. This is the

practice of facing our own fear. Fear is always there within us—the fear of getting old, the fear of getting sick, the fear of dying, the fear of being abandoned by our loved ones. It is very human to be fearful and to worry about it.

The Buddha did not advise us to suppress these fears. The Buddha advised us to invite these fears to the upper level of our consciousness, recognize them and smile at them. To do so was a daily practice for monks and nuns in the time of the Buddha as it is for monks and nuns now. Every time your fear is invited up, every time you recognize it and smile at it, your fear will lose some of its strength. When it returns to the depth of your consciousness, it returns as a smaller seed. That is why the practice should be done every day, especially when you are feeling mentally and physically strong.

When you try to practice, your mind may be running after many thoughts. But just come back to the awareness of when you are breathing in and when you are breathing out. Just be aware of it—you do not need to make your breath longer or deeper. You do not need to change anything. Allow your breath to be just as it wants to be. Keep your mind with the breath in awareness. After practicing like that, the quality of your breathing will calm itself.

When you feel calm enough, use the words of the guided meditation below to help you concentrate. The first time, you may like to hear or say to yourself the whole sentence. As you continue, you can just remember a few key words.

You do not need to make a big effort. Just relax and let your breath and the words be your support.

EXERCISE TO HELP US LOOK DEEPLY
AND HEAL OUR FEAR

Breathing in, I am aware of my in-breath.	*In*
Breathing out, I am aware of my out-breath.	*Out*
Breathing in, I am aware that I grow old.	*Old age*
Breathing out, I know I cannot escape old age.	*No escape*
Breathing in, I am aware of my nature to have ill health.	*Ill health*
Breathing out, I know I cannot escape ill health.	*No escape*
Breathing in, I know I shall die.	*Death*
Breathing out, I know I cannot escape death.	*No escape*
Breathing in, I know that one day I shall have to abandon all I love and cherish.	*Abandon all I cherish*

Breathing out, I know I cannot escape
abandoning all I cherish.   *No escape*

Breathing in, I know that my actions of
body, speech and mind are my only   *Actions true*
true belongings.   *belongings*

Breathing out, I know I cannot escape the   *No escaping*
consequences of my actions.   *consequences*

Breathing in, I determine to live my days   *Living*
deeply in mindfulness.   *mindfully*

Breathing out, I see the joy and benefit   *Joy and*
of living in the present moment.   *benefit*

Breathing in, I vow to offer joy each day
to my beloved.   *Offering joy*

Breathing out, I vow to ease the pain of
my beloved.   *Easing pain*

Acceptance, forgiveness and facing fear are the deepest
results of Touching the Earth in the historical dimension.
Using the breath this way, we can begin to heal. Then we can
look at the next Touching of the Earth.

Touching the Earth: Space

In the first Touching of the Earth, you practice while visualizing standing on the vertical line of time. Now visualize a horizontal line, which represents the dimension of space. This line representing space crosses the vertical line representing time, the historical dimension.

In space we see other living beings on the planet Earth: men, women, children, elderly people, animals of every species, trees, plants, minerals. When we look at a tree we may think that the tree is outside of us. But if we look more deeply we shall see that the tree is also within us. The trees are your lungs because without the trees you could not breathe. The trees create the oxygen, which is now part of my body, and I create the carbon dioxide, which is now part of the tree. We have lungs in our body, but the trees breathe for us too and can also be called our lungs. Our own lungs are working with the trees to help us breathe.

The Jataka Tales are stories about the lives the Buddha lived before he became enlightened. In those stories we hear how the Buddha was a tree, a bird, a tortoise, a rock, a cloud before he was a human. We too, before manifesting in human form, were trees, one-celled animals, large animals, clouds, forests, rocks. It is not difficult to see in the light of scientific evolution. Matter is neither created nor destroyed. It can change into energy, and energy can change back into matter, but it won't be destroyed.

We have always been a part of everything else, and everything else has always been a part of us. We have all been trees, roses and animals. We still are trees at this moment. Look deeply at yourself and you see the tree, the cloud, the rose and the squirrel in you. You cannot take them out of yourself. You cannot take the cloud out of you because you are made of seventy percent water. The continuation of the cloud is rain. The continuation of rain is the river. The continuation of the river is the water you drink in order to survive. If you take the continuation of the cloud out of you, you cannot continue.

Angels Everywhere

Looking deeply into the dimension of space, we will also see all the enlightened beings. All the great beings, the bodhisattvas. We will see God. Look hard and you will see bodhisattvas everywhere. You will see men and women who have compassion and who do everything they can to help and protect humanity. In Plum Village we practice evoking the names of bodhisattvas such as Avalokiteshvara, the bodhisattva of deep listening; Samantabhadra, the bodhisattva of great action; Manjushri, the bodhisattva of great understanding; Kshitigarbha, the bodhisattva who always goes to the darkest places, where suffering is unbearable, to help all people.

These are the bodhisattvas we know about because their stories have been passed down to us. There are also countless unknown bodhisattvas everywhere whose work expresses their love, compassion and deep commitment to the world. Their hearts are full of love, and they are not interested in consuming many things. They want to live simply in order to have time and energy to support others. They are everywhere. I know a bodhisattva who lives in Holland. Her name is Hebe. During World War II she helped twenty thousand Jews escape the Holocaust. I do not know how she did it. Looking at her you see that she is very small and she only has two hands. I met her and worked with her when she was helping with Vietnamese war orphans.

There are also bodhisattvas who do not seem to be very active, but they are very calm and kind and their presence inspires us with love, understanding and tolerance.

There are countless bodhisattvas like that in the world. We should live so that we have time to recognize and touch their presence. Bodhisattvas are not gods or figures from the past. They are living around you in flesh and blood. They have much energy, understanding and compassion, and we can benefit from being near them.

Great Beings, bodhisattvas, cannot be recognized by their outer appearance. Sometimes they are small children who bring us much joy. Our own children and our friends are bodhisattvas. Sometimes they make us suffer, but they also help us to grow in love and understanding.

The bodhisattvas never grow weary of the suffering around them and never give up. They are the ones who give us the courage to live. Kshitigarbha, who goes into the darkest places to help all beings, is not just one person. He has so many manifestations in all the different hell realms, which we can find right in this world.

Sadaparibhuta, the bodhisattva who says, "I would never dare to despise anyone," is also everywhere. Even if someone does not seem to have the ability to be awakened, he sees that within everyone there is that capacity. Sadaparibhuta helps everyone to have self-confidence and remove any feelings of inferiority. This kind of complex paralyzes people. Sadaparibhuta's specialty is to be in touch with and water the seeds of the awakened mind or the mind of love in us. This bodhisattva is not just a person in the Lotus Sutra but can be found right here in our society in many different guises. We have to recognize the bodhisattva Sadaparibhuta, who is around us in flesh and bones.

Manjushri is the bodhisattva who has understanding—someone who can understand us can make us infinitely happy. Manjushri is able to see our suffering and our difficulties and never blames or punishes us. He is always beside us to encourage us and shine light on us. Manjushri is not a legendary figure but is present around us in many guises, sometimes as a younger sister or brother or nephew or niece.

We do not worship imaginary or mythological figures. Bodhisattvas are not figures from the past living up in the clouds. The bodhisattvas are real people who are filled with love and determination. When we can understand someone else's suffering and feel love for him or her, we are in touch with the bodhisattva of great understanding.

The bodhisattva of deep listening, Avalokiteshvara, is also around us. Psychotherapists have to learn the art of listening as deeply as bodhisattva Avalokiteshvara, the one who looks deeply with her ears. When we can listen deeply to our children or our parents, Avalokiteshvara is already in our hearts.

The bodhisattva of wonderful sound, Gadgadashvara, can use music, writings and sound to awaken people. If you are a poet, a writer or a composer you can be that bodhisattva. Your artistic creations are not just to help people forget their pain momentarily but to water the seeds of awakened understanding and compassion in others. Among us are many writers, poets and composers who are using the wonderful ocean of sound to serve the way of understanding

They have no way to speak out about the suffering and injustice that they have to bear. There are pirates who are raping young girls. There are rich merchants selling arms to poor nations where children do not have food to eat or schools to attend. There are factory owners who use children as their workforce. There are people who are dying in prisons and reeducation camps. In leprosy camps there are children and adults without limbs, illiterate and without hope. These hell realms need bodhisattvas.

When we stand before the mountain or flower and visualize just before we touch the earth the second time, we see that we are not only bodhisattvas but we are also the victims of oppression, discrimination and injustice. With the energy of the bodhisattvas we embrace victims everywhere. We are the pirate about to rape the young girl and we are the young girl who is about to be raped. Because we have no separate selves, we are all interconnected and we are with all of them.

How we live our life affects everything. So we must think, *How have we lived our life so that that young man in Thailand has been able to become a rapist?* We have only looked to our own material needs. The family into which that young man was born has been stuck in miserable poverty for many generations. His father was a fisherman who only knew one way to forget his troubles and that was by drinking. He did not know how to bring up his sons, and he beat them often. His mother did not know how to provide education for her children. At thirteen years old he had to accompany his father on the boat and learn to be a fisherman. When his father died he continued in his father's place. He had no resources of understanding and love. He was tempted to become a pirate because in just one day a pirate can have real gold, which could lift him out of his miserable state that he feared would go on forever. On the ocean there was no police force, so why not follow the example of the other pirates and rape the young girls on the boat they plundered?

If we had a gun we could shoot that young man, and he would die, but would it not have been better to help him to understand and to love? Where were the politicians, the statesmen and the educators to help him?

Last night on the shores of Thailand hundreds of babies were born to fishing families. If those children are not properly cared for, brought up and educated, some of them will become pirates. Whose fault is that? It is our fault: statesmen, politicians, the electorate who puts them in power and the educators. We cannot blame only that young man. If I had been born a poor child who was never educated, who had a mother and a father who were illiterate, who had been poor all their lives and did not know how to bring me up, I could have become a pirate. If you were to shoot me dead, would it solve anything? Who is that pirate? He could be me, and the child he raped could also be me.

All the suffering of living beings is our own suffering.

We have to see that we are they and they are us. When we see their suffering, an arrow of compassion and love enters our hearts. We can love them, embrace them and find a way to help. Only then are we not overwhelmed by despair at their situation. Or our own.

Don't Drown in Despair

When you are in touch with the suffering in the world, it is so easy for despair to overwhelm you. But we do not need to be drowned by despair. Throughout the war in Vietnam young people easily became the victims of despair because the war went on for so long and it seemed it would never end. It is the same with the situation in the Middle East. Young Israelis and Palestinians feel that the heavy atmosphere of war will never end. We have to practice to protect our children and ourselves from despair. Bodhisattvas can stand up and resist despair by their ability to listen deeply, to love, to understand and to be deeply committed. As we touch the Earth the second time we are in contact with great and small bodhisattvas everywhere, and we feel their energy.

Animals, plants and minerals also suffer because of the greed of human beings. The earth, the water and the air are suffering because we have polluted them. The trees suffer because we destroy the forests for our own profit. Some species have become extinct because of the destruction of the natural environment. Humans also destroy and exploit one another. According to the teachings of Buddhism, all beings have the capacity of awakened nature. How can we stop ourselves from collapsing in despair? It is because Buddhas and bodhisattvas are present in the world. They are not somewhere else in a faraway paradise. Whether we are living or dying, they are here, with us.

Benefiting Everyone

Touching the Earth helps us to purify our bodies and our minds. It helps us to maintain the awakened understanding of impermanence, interconnectedness and no self. The Buddha has said that whoever sees inter-being sees the Buddha. So as we touch the earth we see Buddhas in us and we see ourselves in the Buddhas. We see all suffering beings in us and we see ourselves in them. As we keep the prostrate position, the boundary between self and other is removed. Then we know what we should do and should not do in our daily lives. Because of this insight, we can do many things of great benefit.

What have you done with your life? Has what you have done been of real benefit to yourself, your loved ones and all beings?

The deep commitment of the bodhisattva is to relieve

suffering. It is to make a career out of becoming an Awakened One, a Buddha. When we make the decision to have our career be that of the bodhisattva, we can let go of all the meaningless things that had attracted us before. We can let go of fame, we can let go of having a lot of money. When we make the decision, those things are easy to let go of.

The Buddhas are in us; we are in the Buddhas. We can become Buddhas. We can become enlightened.

Guiding Ourselves

Use the following words to guide you in the beginning of your practice of the second touching:

"Touching the earth, I connect with all people and all species that are alive at this moment in this world with me." (*Visualize for a short time standing before your preferred object, before you touch the earth.*)

I am one with the wonderful pattern of life that radiates out in all directions. I see the close connection between others and myself, how our happiness and suffering is interconnected. I am one with those bodhisattvas and great beings who have overcome the ideas of birth and death and are able to look compassionately at the different forms of birth and death without fear. I am one with those bodhisattvas who can be found in many places on this planet. They have peace of mind, understanding and love. They are able to touch what is wonderful, nourishing and healing, and bring it to others. They have the capacity to embrace the world with a heart of love and arms of caring action. I too am someone who has enough peace, joy and freedom to be able to offer fearlessness and joy to those around me. I do not feel loneliness or despair when I feel the love and the happiness of bodhisattvas presently alive on this earth. Seeing their love and seeing the suffering of all beings helps me to live in a meaningful way with true peace and happiness.

Strengthened by the love of bodhisattvas, I am able to see myself in all the beings who suffer. I am one with those who were born disabled or who have become disabled because of war, accident or illness. I am one with those who are caught in a situation of war or oppression. I am one with those who find no happiness in family life, who have no roots or peace of mind, who are hungry for something beautiful and wholesome to embrace and to believe in. I am someone at the point of death who is very afraid, who does not know what is going to happen and fears being destroyed. I am a child who lives in a place where there is miserable poverty and disease, whose legs and arms are like sticks, and who has no future. I am also the manufacturer of bombs, which are sold to poor countries. I am the frog swimming in the pond and I am also the snake who needs the body of the frog to nourish its own body. I am the caterpillar or the ant that the bird is looking for to eat, but

I am also the bird that is looking for the insect to eat. I am the forest that is being cut down. I am the rivers that are being polluted, and I am the person who cuts down the forest and pollutes the rivers and the air. I see myself in all beings and I see all beings in me.

Looking Deeply at No Birth and No Death

When we begin to understand that we are everything, our fear begins to disappear. We have deeply touched the dimensions of space and time. But to really be free of fear, we must look deeply into the ultimate dimension of no birth, no death. We need to free ourselves from these ideas that we are our body, and that we die. This is where we will discover the place of no fear. This is the third Touching of the Earth. Here is a guided meditation to help you prepare for it.

Breathing in, I know that I am
breathing in.   *In*

Breathing out, I know that I am
breathing out.   *Out*

Breathing in, I am aware of a wave on
the ocean.   *Wave*

Breathing out, I smile to the wave on
the ocean.   *I smile*

Breathing in, I am aware of the water in   *Water*
the wave.   *in wave*

Breathing out, I smile to the water in
the wave.   *I smile*

Breathing in, I see the birth of the wave.   *Birth of wave*

Breathing out, I smile to the birth of
the wave.   *I smile*

Breathing in, I see the death of the wave.   *Death*
                                                             of wave

Breathing out, I smile to the death of
the wave.   *I smile*

Breathing in, I see the birthless nature   *Water*
of the water.   *not born*

Breathing out, I smile to the birthless
nature of the wave.   *I smile*

Breathing in, I see the deathless nature of   *Water*
the water.   *deathless*

Breathing out, I smile to the deathless
nature of the water.   *I smile*

Breathing in, I see the birth of my body.   *Birth of*
                                                                    my body

Breathing out, I smile to the birth of my
body.   *I smile*

Breathing in, I see the death of my body.   *My body*
                                                                    dies

Breathing out, I smile to the death of
my body.   *I smile*

Breathing in, I see the birthless nature of   *Birthless*
my body.   *nature*
                                                                    of body

Breathing out, I smile to the birthless
nature of my body.   *I smile*

Breathing in, I see the deathless nature of   *Deathless*
my body.   *nature*
                                                                    of body

Breathing out, I smile to the deathless
nature of my body.   *I smile*

Breathing in, I see the birthless nature of my consciousness.	*Consciousness not born*
Breathing out, I smile to the birthless nature of consciousness.	*I smile*
Breathing in, I am only aware of my in-breath.	*In*
Breathing out, I am only aware of my out-breath.	*Out*

I Am Not My Body

When I was a novice I thought that the business of going beyond birth and death was something very remote. I thought I would never be able to realize it in one lifetime. But birth and death are just ideas. All we need to do is overcome these ideas. When I learned that, I saw that such a feat was not impossible. These two ideas have imprisoned us for so many lifetimes.

Now we see that we are more than our bodies. Now we see that we have no life spans. We have no limits. We experience this in meditation. If we have been successful in the first and second Touching of the Earth, this third touching is as simple as a child's game.

The third Touching of the Earth is like a circle placed around the vertical line of time in the first touching and the horizontal line of space in the second touching. In the first touching, we were released from the view that we are separate from our ancestors and separate from our descendants. We were released from our notion of time. In the second touching, we were released from the view that we are separate from the Buddhas, the bodhisattvas, the Great Beings, the suffering beings, the animals, the plants, everything. We were released from our notion of space. This time we touch the earth and are released from the view that we are our body, and that we are subject to birth and death.

Generally, we think that we are our bodies. We think that when our bodies disintegrate, we disintegrate. The Buddha taught clearly that we are not this body.

I often ask my young friends who are not yet thirty years old, "Where were you in 1966 when I left Vietnam?" They should not reply that they did not yet exist. They have to see that they were around, in their parents and their grandparents.

You can use the following words to guide you in your initial practice of the third touching: "Touching the Earth, I let go of the idea that I am this body and my life span is limited." (*Standing before your preferred object, visualize for a short time before you touch the Earth.*)

I see that this body, made up of the four elements, is not

really me and I am not limited by this body. I am part of a stream of life of spiritual and blood ancestors that for thousands of years has been flowing into the present and for thousands of years flows on into the future. I am one with my ancestors. I am one with all people and all beings, whether they are peaceful and fearless or suffering and afraid. At this moment I am present everywhere on this planet. I am also present in the past and in the future. The disintegration of this body does not touch me, just as when the plum blossom falls it does not mean the end of the plum tree. I see myself as a wave on the surface of the ocean. My nature is the ocean water. I see myself in all the other waves and all the other waves in me. The appearance and disappearance of the form of the wave does not affect the ocean. My dharma body and wisdom life are not subject to birth and death. I see the presence of myself before my body manifested and after my body has disintegrated. Even in this moment I see how I exist elsewhere than in this body. Seventy or eighty years is not my life span. My life span, like the life span of a leaf or of a Buddha, is limitless. I have gone beyond the idea that I am a body that is separated in space and time.

Those of you who have touched things deeply in the dimension of space and time will be able to touch this ultimate dimension. After you have touched the wave, you learn to touch the water.

No Separation

The Buddha said the nature of your reality is the nature of no birth and no death; no coming, no going; no being, no non-being; no same, no different. This teaching sounds as though it contradicts the teaching that everything that is born must die, the teaching that we cannot escape death, sickness and old age. Practice looking deeply. You will realize that birth is a notion, death is a notion, coming is a notion, going is a notion, being is a notion and non-being is also a notion. We have to remove all notions concerning reality. Then we touch the ultimate reality, or suchness.

Suchness is a technical term. It means that reality is as it is. You cannot say anything about it; you cannot describe it. You can say that God is the ultimate reality and anything that can be said about God is wrong. Any notion, any idea concerning God cannot describe God. Nirvana is the same. Nirvana is the removal of all notions and concepts so that reality can reveal herself fully to you. In the historical dimension, observing a wave, we can talk about the birth of the wave, the death of the wave, the wave as being high or low, more or less beautiful, this wave and that wave, and so on. Concerning the ultimate dimension, water, all the adjectives, all the ideas that you use to describe the wave, are no longer valid. There is no birth, no death; no this, no that; no high, no low; no more beautiful, no less beautiful. The wave does not have to die in order to become water. The wave is water in this very moment.

Practice this now so that you do not feel separated from your loved one when she dies. If you have deep insight, you will not feel abandoned. Every day I look deeply at everything around me: the trees, the hills, my friends. I see myself in them all and I know I shall not die. I will continue in many other forms. When my friends look at me they should see me in forms other than this visible body. This daily practice will help them not to cry when the moment comes for my present manifestation to disappear. For when this manifestation disappears, it will leave room for other manifestations.

Nine

ACCOMPANYING
THE DYING

Anathapindika was a very dear lay disciple of the Buddha. He was from the kingdom of Koshala, north of the Ganga River in the foothills of the Himalayan Mountains. Anathapindika was a successful and respected merchant and businessman. He was beloved by his countrymen for his generous heart. His real name was Sudatta, but he was given the honorary title Anathapindika, meaning, "the one who takes care of the destitute." This was in appreciation for his tireless efforts in supporting poor people, orphans and the homeless.

One day when he was about thirty years old, he traveled on business to the kingdom of Magadha, where the Buddha also happened to be staying. When he arrived in Magadha, he went first to visit his younger sister and her husband, who were living there at the time. He was surprised when he was not greeted with the customary ceremony and attention. When he asked his sister why she was not spending any time with him, she replied that the entire household was busy preparing to receive a wonderful teacher who was called the Buddha. Upon hearing the name of the Buddha, he was very curious. He asked his sister, "Who is that?" She answered by speaking so respectfully about the Buddha that it inspired him to want to go and see the Buddha as soon as possible.

Early the next day Anathapindika went to the Bamboo Grove Monastery, where the Buddha was speaking. The talk moved him deeply. Bowing to the Earth, Anathapindika invited the Buddha to come to his hometown to share the teaching and practice with his friends and family.

Although this was only the third year of the Buddha's ministry, he already had more than one thousand two hundred monastic disciples. Among the monks traveling with the Buddha was the Venerable Shariputra. Shariputra had already been a well-known spiritual teacher before he became a student of the Buddha. When Shariputra became a disciple of the Buddha, all his younger dharma brothers and students joined him.

The Buddha accepted Anathapindika's invitation to go to Shravasti, which was the capital city of the kingdom of Koshala. Anathapindika went ahead to prepare for the Buddha's visit. He needed a monk to accompany him home to help. The Buddha asked the Venerable Shariputra, who was very talented in building community, to go with him. Shariputra and Anathapindika, one monk and one layperson, soon became very close friends.

Some people think that only monastics can be close to monastics and that only laypeople can be close to laypeople. But this is not so. If both monastics and laypeople are motivated by a deep desire to practice the mindfulness trainings and to look deeply, they can be very intimate friends, co-workers and copractitioners. There is no discrimination. A monk can be a good monk, a layperson can be a good layperson, and they can also be close friends.

Anathapindika wanted to offer the Buddha a piece of property on which to build a monastery in Koshala. After looking extensively, he felt there was only one place beautiful enough. It was a lovely park belonging to a member of the royal family of Koshala, the Prince Jeta. Since Anathapindika was very wealthy, he thought he could convince the prince to sell him this property. The prince had planted many beautiful trees on the property, so it was much more than a piece of land—it was like a paradise. When Anathapindika came to the prince and asked to buy the land, the prince refused. Anathapindika offered more money, and still the prince refused. In the end Anathapindika said: "How much do you want for it? I am ready to pay any amount." The prince replied, "If you can cover all the land with gold leaf, then I will sell it to you." When the prince said this, he was actually joking. He never believed that Anathapindika would accept his proposal, but he did.

Anathapindika soon brought enough gold leaf to cover the whole area of land. The prince still did not want to sell it, but his advisors said: "You must sell it. You are a prince of the royal family. You've already given your word and you cannot break it."

Prince Jeta found it difficult to understand that a spiritual teacher could be so extraordinary and that Anathapindika could respect and love him so much that he would pay such a huge sum to buy a piece of land as a gift. People told the prince that the Buddha, who was still a young teacher, was fully awakened and that his teachings and his compassion were beyond compare. Seeing the great faith and admiration of Anathapindika, Prince Jeta stopped him just before he had covered all of the land and said: "You've given me so much gold already. That's enough. I want to offer to the Buddha the trees I have planted on the land as a gift from myself to the Buddha." That is why the place is called the Anathapindika Jeta Grove. It was land purchased and given to the Buddha by Anathapindika, but the trees were given by Prince Jeta. The Buddha loved this park very much and spent twenty consecutive annual rainy-season retreats there. You can visit the park still and see the archaeological remains of ancient Buddhist monasteries.

All during the years following his meeting with the Buddha, Anathapindika continued his work helping the poor and supporting the Buddha, the dharma and the sangha. He was the Buddha's good friend as was the king of Koshala.

Anathapindika had a lovely family, and his wife and two children also became students of the Buddha. The entire family came every week to the Jeta Grove to hear dharma talks and enjoy the practice of mindfulness. Often Anathapindika would bring fellow businessmen to meet the Buddha and receive his teachings. On one famous occasion, he brought more than five hundred businessmen to the Jeta Grove, where the Buddha gave a dharma talk on practice of mindfulness for laypeople. Most of the friends of Anathapindika accepted the five mindfulness trainings. Throughout his life, Anathapindika took a great deal of pleasure and happiness in supporting the Buddha, the dharma and the sangha.

Although throughout his life he experienced many successes, there were also many difficult moments in his life. One time he lost his entire fortune, but with the help of his employees and friends he was able to rebuild his business and his wealth.

Thirty-five years after his first meeting with the Buddha, he fell very ill. Hearing of his sickness, the Buddha came to visit him and urged him to practice mindful breathing while lying in bed. Then the Buddha charged the Venerable Shariputra with taking good care of his old friend. The Buddha asked Shariputra to remain in Koshala with Anathapindika and to help him die peacefully.

When Shariputra learned that Anathapindika was fast approaching death, he asked his younger brother in the dharma, the Venerable Ananda, to go with him to see his old friend. Ananda was a cousin of the Buddha and had memorized all the Buddha's dharma talks. He is one of the main reasons we have the teachings of the Buddha today.

After finishing their daily alms round, the two of them went to the house of Anathapindika. When the two monks arrived, Anathapindika, who needed them very much in this difficult moment, was happy to see them. He tried his best to sit up and greet them in a proper manner, but he could not because he was so weak.

Shariputra said to him, "My dear friend, don't try to sit up; just lie down and we will bring two chairs and sit close to you." Then, Shariputra asked, "Dear friend, how do you feel in your body? Do you feel pain? If so, is it increasing or is it decreasing?"

Anathapindika answered, "Dear friend, it does not seem that the pain in my body is decreasing. It seems it is increasing all the time."

Shariputra then said, "In that case, I suggest we practice a guided meditation on the Three Jewels." He began to offer a meditation on the Buddha, the dharma and the sangha, with the support of the Venerable Ananda sitting beside him. Shariputra was considered to be one of the most brilliant monastic disciples of the Buddha. He was like the right arm of the Buddha. He was the elder brother to thousands of monks and nuns. He knew that Anathapindika had gotten a great deal of pleasure over the years serving the Buddha, the dharma and the sangha. He also knew that for Anathapindika this meditation would water seeds of happiness in him at that difficult moment.

He shared with Anathapindika the practice of recollecting the wonderful nature of the Buddha, the dharma and the sangha. In just five or six minutes the pain that Anathapindika felt throughout his body lessened as the seeds of happiness in him were watered. His balance was restored. Anathapindika smiled.

Watering the seeds of happiness is a very important practice for the sick or dying. All of us have seeds of happiness inside us, and in difficult moments when we are sick or when we are dying, there should be a friend sitting with us to help us touch the seeds of happiness within. Otherwise seeds of fear, of regret or of despair can easily overwhelm us.

When Anathapindika was able to smile, Shariputra knew that the balance between the joy and pain in him had been restored. He invited Anathapindika to continue the guided meditation. He said, "Dear friend, please practice together with Ananda and myself as follows. Breathing in, I see that this body is not me. Breathing out, I am not caught in this body. I am life without limit. I have never been born and I will never die."

When you are about to die, you may not be very aware of your body. You may experience some numbness, and yet you are caught in the idea that this body is you. You are caught in the notion that the disintegration of this body is your own disintegration. That is why you are fearful. You are afraid you are becoming nothing. The disintegration of his body cannot affect the dying person's true nature. You have to explain to him that he is life without limit. This body is just a manifestation, like a cloud. When a cloud is no longer a cloud, it is not lost. It has not become nothing; it has transformed; it has become rain. Therefore we should not identify our self with our body. *This body is not me. I am not caught in this body. I am life without limit.*

In fact, we have to begin this practice with our eyes, nose, ears, tongue, body and mind: "These eyes are not me. I am not caught in these eyes. I am life without boundaries. These ears are not me. I am not caught in these ears. I am life without limit. This nose is not me, I am not caught in this nose and I am life without boundaries." This practice helps us not to identify ourselves with our eyes, ears, nose, tongue and body. We explore each sense consciousness and each sense organ so that we can see that we are not them. We are much more than the manifestation of our sense organs. The cessation of the manifestations does not affect us.

Then we look at and see what else we might think is our identity. Beyond the body and the senses are the five aggregates of form, feelings, perceptions, mental formations and consciousness. We have to look deeply at each one and say, "These things are not me." Perceptions, feelings, ideas come and go. They cannot be me. Consciousness, just like perceptions, feelings and mental formations, is just a manifestation. When conditions are sufficient, these manifestations are present. When conditions are no longer sufficient, these manifestations are no longer present. Present or not present, these manifestations are not me.

Shariputra guided Anathapindika through the sense consciousnesses and the five aggregates, and Anathapindika saw that they were not him. So Shariputra began the guided meditation on the Four Elements. He said to Anathapindika, "Dear friend, let us continue our meditation. The element earth in me is not me. (Here 'earth' means everything that is solid: flesh, bones, muscles and organs.) The fire element or the heat to keep warm and digest food is not me. I am not caught in the fire element or the heat in me. The water element in me is not me. There is water everywhere in and around me. I am free of the element water. The air element in me is not me because I am life without boundaries." Shariputra continued like that.

Finally, Anathapindika was guided in the meditation on Interdependent Origination. "Dear friend, let us look more deeply. When conditions are sufficient, my body manifests itself. It does not come from anywhere, and after disintegration it does not go anywhere." When things manifest, we cannot really call them being. When things stop their manifestation, we cannot really describe them as non-being. We are free from notions of coming, going, being, non-being, birth, death, same and different. It was exactly the kind of practice and teaching that we understand when we contemplate a cloud, a flame or the sunflowers.

When he had practiced to that point, Anathapindika began to cry. Ananda was surprised. Venerable Ananda was much younger than Shariputra, and he was not able to see the transformation and liberation Anathapindika had undergone in those few moments. He thought Anathapindika was crying because he regretted something or did not succeed in his meditation. Ananda asked, "Dear friend, why are you crying? Do you regret anything?"

Anathapindika said, "No, Venerable Ananda, I don't regret anything."

Ananda then asked, "Maybe your practice was not successful?"

Anathapindika replied, "No Venerable Ananda, it was very successful."

Ananda asked, "Then why are you crying?"

Anathapindika answered with tears in his eyes, "Venerable Ananda, I am crying because I am so moved. I have served the sangha, the dharma and the Buddha for thirty-five years and yet I have never received and practiced such wonderful teachings as these the Venerable Shariputra has given me today. I am so happy! I am so free!"

Ananda then said to him, "Dear friend, you may not know it, but we monks and nuns receive this kind of teaching almost every day."

Anathapindika smiled and in his feeble voice said quietly, "Dear Venerable Ananda, please go back to the monastery and tell the Lord Buddha that I do understand that many laypeople are so busy and that they will not make the time to receive and practice this kind of teaching. But there are many of us who are free enough and are available enough to receive this teaching and this practice. Please ask the Lord Buddha to dispense this teaching and this practice to us, the laypeople also."

Knowing that this was the last request of Anathapindika, the Venerable Ananda answered him, "Of course I will do as you ask. I will tell the Lord Buddha as soon as I return to the Jeta Grove." Shortly after the visit of the two monks, Anathapindika died peacefully and without pain.

This story is recorded in a discourse called "The Teachings to be Given to the Dying."* I would like to advise anyone who is able to please study the discourse and to practice it. Please do not wait until you have to face the problem of dying in order to study and practice it. Please practice looking deeply now in order to touch your nature of no birth, no death; no coming, no going; no same, no different. If you do so, you will stop your grief and suffering. If you do this practice with diligence and effort, you will nurture the element of non-fear in you. You will be able to die happily and peacefully.

It is very possible to live happily and to die peacefully. We do this by seeing that we continue our manifestation in other forms. It is also possible to help others to die peacefully if we have the elements of solidity and non-fear in us. So many of us are afraid of non-being. Because of this fear, we suffer a lot. That is why the reality that we are a manifestation and a con-

* Ibid., 267.

tinuation of many manifestations should be revealed to the dying person. We are then not affected by the fear of birth and death, because we understand that these are just notions. This is a very important insight that can liberate us from fear.

I have taken the words and teachings from the sutra to be "Given to the Dying" in the *Anguttara Nikaya* and made them into a song. It is a lullaby song that can be sung to the person who is nearing their last breath:

> *This body is not me; I am not caught in this body,*
> *I am life without boundaries,*
> *I have never been born and I have never died.*
> *Over there the wide ocean and the sky with many galaxies*
> *All manifests from the basis of consciousness.*
> *Since beginningless time I have always been free.*
> *Birth and death are only a door through which we go in and out.*
> *Birth and death are only a game of hide-and-seek.*
> *So smile to me and take my hand and wave good-bye.*
> *Tomorrow we shall meet again or even before.*
> *We shall always be meeting again at the true source,*
> *Always meeting again on the myriad paths of life.*

The first line can be repeated with *These eyes . . . These ears . . . This nose . . . This tongue . . . This mind . . . These forms . . . These sounds . . . etc.* instead of *This body* (e.g., *These eyes are not me; I am not caught in these eyes . . .*)

Singing this song to a dying person can help them be free from thinking that they have a permanent identity that is connected to any part of the body or mind. All things that are composite decompose, but our true selves do not disappear into oblivion. This kind of guided meditation helps us to avoid being caught in the idea that we are this body, we are this thought, and we are this emotion. We are actually not these things. We are life without limit. We are not caught in birth, we are not caught in death, we are not caught in being, and we are not caught in non-being. This is the truth of reality.

So please do not be too busy in your daily life. Please take time to practice. Learn how to live happily, peacefully and joyfully today. Please learn the practice of looking deeply and understanding the true nature of birth and death so you can die peacefully and without fear. This is something everyone can do.

If you can practice so that you have no fear, when one of your friends or dear ones is dying, you will be able to help them. You have to know what you really need to do and what you really do not need to do. You are intelligent enough to be able to use your time skillfully. You do not need to waste your time doing those things that are unnecessary and trifling. You do not have to be rich. You do not need to seek fame or power. What you need is freedom, solidity, peace and joy. You need the time and energy to be able to share these things with others.

Our happiness does not rely on our having a lot of money

or fame. Our security comes from whether we practice and keep the mindfulness trainings. Once we have the mindfulness trainings and the Buddha, the dharma and the sangha looking after us, we are happy. Our two eyes are bright, our smile is fresh, and our steps are solidly on the path of a free life. Our happiness flows over to those around us. We do not give our time to things that are superficial. We use our time to practice so that the quality of our lives will be better. This is the most precious gift any of us can leave our children or our grand-children. This is the best that we can share with our friends. We need time to receive, practice and learn about the wonder-ful teachings of the Buddha, like those taught to Anathapin-dika at the time of his death.

Taking refuge in our family, friends and community, in the sangha, we change our way of life. We have to live with peace and joy right away and not wait for the future to do it. We have to be well right now, right here, peaceful and joy-ful in the present moment. There is no way to happiness—happiness is the way.

The teaching given by Shariputra should be given to everyone early on in life. Anathapindika was very lucky to re-ceive the teaching at the last moment. Things are imperma-nent and we do not know in advance when we shall breathe our last. We may not be as lucky as Anathapindika to have good spiritual friends by our side to guide us in meditation at the time of our death. That is why we should not leave it until it is too late. We should learn the practice right now so that we will be able to guide ourselves.

A New Story of Dying

In the early 1990s I was on my way to the Omega Institute in upstate New York to lead a retreat when I learned that an old friend of ours was dying in a hospital just north of New York City. His name was Alfred Hassler. He had been director of the Fellowship of Reconciliation. In 1966 and 1967, he and I had traveled together to many countries, organizing efforts to end the war in Vietnam.

Later, I was no longer allowed to go back to Vietnam because I had spoken out in the West against the violation of human rights by both warring parties, North and South. Alfred went to Vietnam in my place to help coordinate the peace work there. He helped support our friends in setting up camps to take care of refugees and victims of the war. We together sponsored more than eight thousand orphans. When I came to the United States in 1966, it was the Fellowship of Reconciliation that organized my first speaking tour. On that tour, I called for an end to the war in Vietnam.

When Sister Chan Khong and I arrived at the hospital, Alfred was already in a coma. Dorothy, his wife, and Laura, his daughter, were there with him. Laura Hassler had volunteered with us at the office of the Vietnamese Buddhist Peace Delegation in Paris when she was very young.

When Dorothy and Laura saw us, they were very happy. Laura tried her best to call Alfred back from his coma. "Daddy, Daddy, Thay is here! Sister Chan Khong is here," she said. But Alfred didn't come back; he was in a very deep coma. I asked Sister Chan Khong to sing to him. A dying person has the capacity to hear, even though we may not realize it. So Sister Chan Khong sang the song that begins, "This body is not me, I am not caught in this body, I am life without boundaries, I have never been born, I will never die." She sang it a second time and again for a third time. In the middle of the third time, Alfred awoke and opened his eyes.

Laura was so happy! She said, "Daddy, do you know that Thay is here? Do you know that Sister Chan Khong is here?" Alfred could not say anything. Looking into his eyes, we felt that he knew we where there. Sister Chan Khong began to talk to him about the experiences we had working together for peace in Vietnam: "Alfred, remember the time you were in Saigon trying to see the monk Tri Quang? The U.S. had decided to bomb Hanoi the day before, and the Venerable Tri Quang was so angry that he vowed not to see any Westerners, either doves or hawks.

"When you arrived he refused to open the door. Alfred, do you remember that you sat there and wrote a note that said, 'I have come as a friend to help stop the war in your country, and not as an enemy. I will not eat anything or drink anything until you open the door for me!' You slipped the note under the door. You remember that? You said, 'I will sit here until you open the door.' Do you remember? Just fifteen minutes later he opened the door. He smiled with a broad smile and invited you in. Alfred, remember the time you were in Rome, and there was a vigil conducted by three hundred Catholic priests, each one bearing the name of a Buddhist monk who had been imprisoned in Saigon for refusing the draft?" Sister Chan Khong continued to talk to him about the happiness we experienced during the time we were working for peace. It had a wonderful effect. She tried to do exactly what Shariputra did for Anathapindika. She was watering the seeds of happiness in him. Alfred's happiness was made of his intention to serve peace and to end suffering for others. When those seeds of happiness were watered, it restored a balance between the joy and the pain in him. He suffered much less.

At that time I was massaging his feet. I was thinking that when a person is dying he might not be very aware of his body because the body is somehow numb. Laura asked, "Daddy, do you know that Thay is massaging your feet?" He didn't say anything but looking into his eyes we were sure that he knew we were there. Suddenly he opened his mouth and said, "Wonderful, wonderful!" After that he sank into a coma again and never came back.

That night I had to give an orientation talk to the retreatants at Omega. We said good-bye and told Dorothy and Laura that they should do as Sister Chan Khong and I had been doing: talking and singing to Alfred. The next morning I received a message from Dorothy telling us that Alfred had died quite peacefully a few hours after we left.

Those who are unconscious have a way to hear us if we are truly present and peaceful as we sit by their bedside. Ten years ago a university student living in Bordeaux heard that his mother was dying in California, and he cried a lot. He did not know if when he arrived home in California his mother would still be alive. Sister Chan Khong told him to fly to California immediately and that if his mother was still alive when he arrived, he should practice just as Shariputra had practiced with Anathapindika. She told him that he should speak about the happy experiences mother and son had shared together. He was to recount stories from her early married life and her youthful years. He should tell her these stories because they would bring her joy, even if she were not conscious.

When he arrived in the hospital, she was already unconscious. Although he did not wholly believe that an unconscious person could hear, he nevertheless did as Sister Chan Khong had instructed him. The doctors told him that his mother had been unconscious for a week and they had no hope that she would regain consciousness before she died. After he had talked to her lovingly for one and a half hours, she woke up.

When you sit by the bedside of a dying person and you are

calm and totally present in body, mind and soul, you will be successful in helping that person pass away in freedom.

A few years ago, Sister Chan Khong had to visit her elder sister in the hospital after a complication from a liver transplant. After two years, her body was rejecting the liver. She was in terrible pain. When Sister Chan Khong walked into the hospital, she saw that everyone in the family had given up all hope of being able to do anything. Although her sister was unconscious, she was still writhing, groaning and screaming in terrible pain. All her children, even her daughter who was a doctor, felt powerless.

Sister Chan Khong arrived at the hospital with a cassette tape of the monks and nuns of Plum Village chanting the name of the bodhisattva Avalokiteshvara, the bodhisattva of great compassion. Although her sister was unconscious, Sister Chan Khong put the cassette tape in the tape player next to the bed and, after putting the headphones on her sister's ears, turned the volume near maximum. Five or six minutes later, something amazing happened. Her sister lay completely quiet. She was no longer writhing, groaning or screaming. She stayed peaceful like that until she passed away five days later.

Throughout those five days, Sister Chan Khong's sister continued to listen to the recitation of the name of the bodhisattva. She had visited Buddhist temples many times and had heard the recitation of the name of the bodhisattva of compassion often. Hearing it again on her deathbed watered

the seeds in her of that which was most precious and joyful while she was alive. She had a spiritual dimension to her life and she had faith. She had heard sutra recitations and listened to teachings of the dharma many times. The cassette tape playing the chanting of the monks and nuns had reached those seeds of happiness. They were seeds that the doctors did not know how to touch. Anyone could have done what Sister Chan Khong did, but no one had thought to do it.

Our consciousness is like a television with many channels. When we push the button on the remote control, the channel we choose appears. When we sit by the bedside of a dying person, we have to know which channel to call up. Those who are closest to the dying person are in the best position to do this. If you are accompanying someone who is dying, use those sounds and images from the life of the person that will water the seeds of their greatest happiness. In the consciousness of everyone are the seeds of the Pure Land and of nirvana, of the kingdom of God and of paradise.

If we know how to practice and penetrate the reality of no birth and no death, if we realize that coming and going are just ideas, and if our presence is solid and peaceful, we can help the dying person. We can help the person not be scared and not to suffer much. We can help the person die peacefully. We can help ourselves live without fear and die peacefully. We can help ourselves to understand that there is no dying. To see that there is no death and there is no fear. There is only continuation.